DOGMATICS

IN

OUTLINE

harper ⚜ torchbooks

American Studies: General

CARL N. DEGLER: Out of Our Past: *The Forces that Shaped Modern America*   CN/2

ROBERT L. HEILBRONER: The Limits of American Capitalism   TB/1305

JOHN HIGHAM, Ed.: The Reconstruction of American History   TB/1068

JOHN F. KENNEDY: A Nation of Immigrants. *Illus. Revised and Enlarged. Introduction by Robert F. Kennedy*   TB/1118

GUNNAR MYRDAL: An American Dilemma: *The Negro Problem and Modern Democracy. Introduction by the Author.*
Vol. I TB/1443; Vol. II TB/1444

GILBERT OSOFSKY, Ed.: The Burden of Race: *A Documentary History of Negro-White Relations in America*   TB/1405

ARNOLD ROSE: The Negro in America: *The Condensed Version of Gunnar Myrdal's An American Dilemma*   TB/3048

American Studies: Colonial

BERNARD BAILYN: The New England Merchants in the Seventeenth Century   TB/1149

ROBERT E. BROWN: Middle-Class Democracy and Revolution in Massachusetts, 1691–1780. *New Introduction by Author*   TB/1413

JOSEPH CHARLES: The Origins of the American Party System   TB/1049

American Studies: The Revolution to 1900

GEORGE M. FREDRICKSON: The Inner Civil War: *Northern Intellectuals and the Crisis of the Union*   TB/1358

WILLIAM W. FREEHLING: Prelude to Civil War: *The Nullification Controversy in South Carolina, 1816-1836*   TB/1359

HELEN HUNT JACKSON: A Century of Dishonor: *The Early Crusade for Indian Reform.* ‡ *Edited by Andrew F. Rolle*   TB/3063

RICHARD B. MORRIS, Ed.: Alexander Hamilton and the Founding of the Nation. *New Introduction by the Editor*   TB/1448

RICHARD B. MORRIS: The American Revolution Reconsidered   TB/1363

GILBERT OSOFSKY, Ed.: Puttin' On Ole Massa: *The Slave Narratives of Henry Bibb, William Wells Brown, and Solomon Northup* †   TB/1432

American Studies: The Twentieth Century

WILLIAM E. LEUCHTENBURG: Franklin D. Roosevelt and the New Deal: 1932-1940. † *Illus.*   TB/3025

WILLIAM E. LEUCHTENBURG, Ed.: The New Deal: *A Documentary History* +   HR/1354

Asian Studies

WOLFGANG FRANKE: China and the West: *The Cultural Encounter, 13th to 20th Centuries. Trans. by R. A. Wilson*   TB/1326

L. CARRINGTON GOODRICH: A Short History of the Chinese People. *Illus.*   TB/3015

BENJAMIN I. SCHWARTZ: Chinese Communism and the Rise of Mao   TB/1308

Economics & Economic History

PETER F. DRUCKER: The New Society: *The Anatomy of Industrial Order*   TB/1082

ROBERT L. HEILBRONER: The Great Ascent: *The Struggle for Economic Development in Our Time*   TB/3030

W. ARTHUR LEWIS: The Principles of Economic Planning. *New Introduction by the Author*°   TB/1436

Historiography and History of Ideas

J. BRONOWSKI & BRUCE MAZLISH: The Western Intellectual Tradition: *From Leonardo to Hegel*   TB/3001

WILHELM DILTHEY: Pattern and Meaning in History: *Thoughts on History and Society.*° *Edited with an Intro. by H. P. Rickman*   TB/1075

J. H. HEXTER: More's Utopia: *The Biography of an Idea. Epilogue by the Author*   TB/1195

ARTHUR O. LOVEJOY: The Great Chain of Being: *A Study of the History of an Idea*   TB/1009

History: Medieval

F. L. GANSHOF: Feudalism   TB/1058

DENYS HAY: The Medieval Centuries °   TB/1192

HENRY CHARLES LEA: A History of the Inquisition of the Middle Ages. || *Introduction by Walter Ullmann*   TB/1456

---

† The New American Nation Series, edited by Henry Steele Commager and Richard B. Morris.
‡ American Perspectives series, edited by Bernard Wishy and William E. Leuchtenburg.
α History of Europe series, edited by J. H. Plumb.
§ The Library of Religion and Culture, edited by Benjamin Nelson.
‖ Researches in the Social, Cultural, and Behavioral Sciences, edited by Benjamin Nelson.
Σ Harper Modern Science Series, edited by James R. Newman.
° Not for sale in Canada.
+ Documentary History of the United States series, edited by Richard B. Morris.
# Documentary History of Western Civilization series, edited by Eugene C. Black and Leonard W. Levy.
Λ The Economic History of the United States series, edited by Henry David et al.
¶ European Perspectives series, edited by Eugene C. Black.
** Contemporary Essays series, edited by Leonard W Levy.
* The Stratum Series, edited by John Hale.

1

History: Renaissance & Reformation

JACOB BURCKHARDT: The Civilization of the Renaissance in Italy. *Introduction by Benjamin Nelson and Charles Trinkaus. Illus.*
Vol. I TB/40; Vol. II TB/41
JOEL HURSTFIELD: The Elizabethan Nation
TB/1312
ALFRED VON MARTIN: Sociology of the Renaissance. ° *Introduction by W. K. Ferguson*
TB/1099
J. H. PARRY: The Establishment of the European Hegemony: 1415-1715: *Trade and Exploration in the Age of the Renaissance* TB/1045

History: Modern European

MAX BELOFF: The Age of Absolutism, 1660-1815
TB/1062
ALAN BULLOCK: Hitler, A Study in Tyranny. ° *Revised Edition. Illus.* TB/1123
JOHANN GOTTLIEB FICHTE: Addresses to the German Nation. *Ed. with Intro. by George A. Kelly* ¶ TB/1366
H. STUART HUGHES: The Obstructed Path: *French Social Thought in the Years of Desperation* TB/1451
JOHAN HUIZINGA: Dutch Cviilization in the 17th Century and Other Essays TB/1453
JOHN MCMANNERS: European History, 1789-1914: *Men, Machines and Freedom* TB/1419
FRANZ NEUMANN: Behemoth: *The Structure and Practice of National Socialism, 1933-1944*
TB/1289
A. J. P. TAYLOR: From Napoleon to Lenin: *Historical Essays* ° TB/1268
H. R. TREVOR-ROPER: Historical Essays TB/1269

Philosophy

HENRI BERGSON: Time and Free Will: *An Essay on the Immediate Data of Consciousness* °
TB/1021
G. W. F. HEGEL: Phenomenology of Mind. ° ‖ *Introduction by George Lichtheim* TB/1303
H. J. PATON: The Categorical Imperative: *A Study in Kant's Moral Philosophy* TB/1325
MICHAEL POLANYI: Personal Knowledge: *Towards a Post-Critical Philosophy* TB/1158
LUDWIG WITTGENSTEIN: The Blue and Brown Books ° TB/1211
LUDWIG WITTGENSTEIN: Notebooks, 1914-1916
TB/1441

Political Science & Government

C. E. BLACK: The Dynamics of Modernization: *A Study in Comparative History* TB/1321
DENIS W. BROGAN: Politics in America. *New Introduction by the Author* TB/1469
KARL R. POPPER: The Open Society and Its Enemies *Vol. I: The Spell of Plato* TB/1101 *Vol: II: The High Tide of Prophecy: Hegel, Marx, and the Aftermath* TB/1102
CHARLES SCHOTTLAND, Ed.: The Welfare State **
TB/1323
JOSEPH A. SCHUMPETER: Capitalism, Socialism and Democracy TB/3008
PETER WOLL, Ed.: Public Administration and Policy: *Selected Essays* TB/1284

Psychology

LUDWIG BINSWANGER: Being-in-the-World: *Selected Papers. ‖ Trans. with Intro. by Jacob Needleman* TB/1365

MIRCEA ELIADE: Cosmos and History: *The Myth of the Eternal Return* § TB/2050
SIGMUND FREUD: On Creativity and the Unconscious: *Papers on the Psychology of Art, Literature, Love, Religion.* § *Intro. by Benjamin Nelson* TB/45
J. GLENN GRAY: The Warriors: *Reflections on Men in Battle. Introduction by Hannah Arendt* TB/1294
WILLIAM JAMES: Psychology: *The Briefer Course. Edited with an Intro. by Gordon Allport* TB/1034

Religion

TOR ANDRAE: Mohammed: *The Man and his Faith* TB/62
KARL BARTH: Church Dogmatics: *A Selection. Intro. by H. Hollwitzer. Ed. by G. W. Bromiley* TB/95
NICOLAS BERDYAEV: The Destiny of Man TB/61
MARTIN BUBER: The Prophetic Faith TB/73
MARTIN BUBER: Two Types of Faith: *Interpenetration of Judaism and Christianity*
TB/75
RUDOLF BULTMANN: History and Eschatalogy: *The Presence of Eternity* TB/91
EDWARD CONZE: Buddhism: *Its Essence and Development. Foreword by Arthur Waley*
TB/58
H. G. CREEL: Confucius and the Chinese Way
TB/63
FRANKLIN EDGERTON, Trans. & Ed.: The Bhagavad Gita TB/115
M. S. ENSLIN: Christian Beginnings TB/5
M. S. ENSLIN: The Literature of the Christian Movement TB/6
HENRI FRANKFORT: Ancient Egyptian Religion: *An Interpretation* TB/77
IMMANUEL KANT: Religion Within the Limits of Reason Alone. *Introduction by Theodore M. Greene and John Silber* TB/67
GABRIEL MARCEL: Homo Viator: *Introduction to a Metaphysic of Hope* TB/397
H. RICHARD NIEBUHR: Christ and Culture TB/3
H. RICHARD NIEBUHR: The Kingdom of God in America TB/49
SWAMI NIKHILANANDA, Trans. & Ed.: The Upanishads TB/114
F. SCHLEIERMACHER: The Christian Faith. *Introduction by Richard R. Niebuhr.*
Vol. I TB/108 Vol. II TB/109

Sociology and Anthropology

KENNETH B. CLARK: Dark Ghetto: *Dilemmas of Social Power. Foreword by Gunnar Myrdal*
TB/1317
KENNETH CLARK & JEANNETTE HOPKINS: A Relevant War Against Poverty: *A Study of Community Action Programs and Observable Social Change* TB/1480
GARY T. MARX: Protest and Prejudice: *A Study of Belief in the Black Community* TB/1435
ROBERT K. MERTON, LEONARD BROOM, LEONARD S. COTTRELL, JR., Editors: Sociology Today: *Problems and Prospects* ‖
Vol. I TB/1173; Vol. II TB/1174
GILBERT OSOFSKY: Harlem: The Making of a Ghetto: *Negro New York, 1890-1930* TB/1381
PHILIP RIEFF: The Triumph of the Therapeutic: *Uses of Faith After Freud* TB/1360
GEORGE ROSEN: Madness in Society: *Chapters in the Historical Sociology of Mental Illness. ‖ Preface by Benjamin Nelson* TB/1337

DOGMATICS
IN
OUTLINE

KARL BARTH

with a new Foreword by the author

HARPER TORCHBOOKS ❦ The Cloister Library

HARPER & ROW, PUBLISHERS
New York

This translation by G. T. Thomson was first published in
1949 by the Student Christian Movement Press, Limited,
London, and is reprinted by arrangement with the Press
and with the Evangelischer Verlag, Zollikon-Zürich, which
published the German original, *Dogmatik im Grundriss*.

First HARPER TORCHBOOK edition published 1959

Library of Congress catalog card number: 59–10343

CONTENTS

Foreword to the Torchbook Edition

MY lectures at the University of Basel are on 'Systematic Theology.' In Basel and elsewhere the juxtaposition of this noun and this adjective is based on a tradition which is quite recent and highly problematic. Is not the term 'Systematic Theology' as paradoxical as a 'wooden iron'? One day this conception will disappear just as suddenly as it has come into being. Nevertheless, even if I allow myself to be called and to be a 'Professor of Systematic Theology,' I could never write a book under this title, as my great contemporary and colleague Tillich has done! A 'system' is an edifice of thought, constructed on certain fundamental conceptions which are selected in accordance with a certain philosophy by a method which corresponds to these conceptions. Theology cannot be carried on in confinement or under the pressure of such a construction. The subject of theology is the history of the communion of God with man and of man with God. This history is proclaimed, in ancient times and today, in the Old and New Testaments. The message of the Christian Church has its origin and its contents in this history. The subject of theology is, in this sense, the 'Word of God.' Theology is a science and a teaching which *feels itself responsible* to the living command of this specific subject and to nothing else in heaven or on earth, in the choice of its methods, its questions and answers, its concepts and language, its goals and limitations. Theology is a free science because it is based on and determined by the kingly freedom of the word of God; for that very reason it can never be 'Systematic Theology.'

In this freedom, theology can be biblical exegesis or research and presentation of the history of the Christian Church, whether or not she was always true to her mandate. It can also be 'practical theology.' The fields of these different disciplines touch and overlap each other. *Dogmatics* is one of these. Directed by the witness of the Old and New Testaments, dogmatic theology is concerned with proving the truth of the message which the Church has always proclaimed and must again proclaim today. It examines the truth contained in certain particular public documents of the past and the present, the *'dogmas.'* Again and again it inquires for the truth from which the proclamation of the Christian Church is derived. For this truth, namely the *'dogma'* which serves as its norm and guide, it searches also today. In doing so it can use many different methods. That is to say, it does not need to be (as in this book) an interpretation of the 'Apostolic' creed. *Methodus est arbitraria.* It only must take care to let

5

itself be directed by God's work and word, on the basis of Holy Writ, and thus to examine *the dogmas* by asking for *the dogma,* so as not to degenerate into 'systematic' theology!

What you will find in this book is merely an *outline* of the multi-volume *Dogmatik.* In the Preface to the original edition you can find details about the strange circumstances under which these lectures originated in Bonn in the summer of 1946. Everything in this *Outline* is treated very concisely. Many important problems of dogmatics are mentioned only briefly or not at all. Therefore, reading this book cannot take the place of studying the *Dogmatik.* At best it can inspire and initiate that study. 'If any one will not work, let him not eat' (II Thess. 3:10, RSV). He who is interested only in the superficial impression given by pleasant or unpleasant catchwords cannot and will not be able to participate in *the truths* (of the dogmas) or *the truth* (of the dogma). The readers of this translation are invited to learn as did the students at Bonn in 1946. He who, after learning a little about the meaning of 'dogmatics,' undertakes to delve more into detail, will, I promise, discover (regardless of the method he may employ) in this theological discipline and in theology in general a great amount of necessary, thrilling, and beautiful tasks which are fruitful for the Church and for the world.

KARL BARTH
translated by Walter M. Mosse

BRIONE IN TESSIN.
March, 1959.

FOREWORD

THESE lectures were delivered in the semi-ruins of the once stately Kurfürsten Schloss in Bonn, in which the University had later been established; the hour seven a.m., always after we had sung a psalm or a hymn to cheer us up. About eight o'clock the rebuilding in the quadrangle began to advertise itself in the rattle of an engine for breaking up the ruins. (I may say that with my inquisitive ways, among the rubbish I came upon an undamaged bust of Schleiermacher, which was rescued and somewhere restored to honour again.) The audience consisted partly of theologians, but the larger part was of students from the other faculties. Most people in the Germany of to-day have in their own way and in their own place endured and survived much, almost beyond all measure. I noted the same in my Bonn lads. With their grave faces, which had still to learn how to smile again, they no less impressed me than I them, I who was an alien, the centre of all sorts of gossip from old times. For me the situation will remain unforgettable. By a mere coincidence it was my fiftieth semester. And when it was past, my impression was that for me it was the best ever.

I really hesitated to publish these lectures as a book. I have already published two paraphrases of the Apostles' Creed, the *Credo* of 1935 and the *Confession de la Foi de l'Église* of 1943. Attentive readers of this book will scarcely discover in this third attempt much that is essentially new; and those who read the larger volumes of the *Kirchliche Dogmatik*, nothing at all. Moreover, for the first time in my life I lectured without a manuscript, and discussed with some freedom the main propositions (here printed in italics at the beginning of each chapter). My return to the primitive conditions which I met with in Germany made it absolutely necessary for me to dispense with a manuscript. The result which is now put before you is a slightly polished and improved shorthand transcript. The reader will miss here and there the precision which I normally strive for, and of course have aimed at here as well. It will be noted especially towards the end that I had to hurry; and that I was preoccupied with

7

other matters besides the lectures. Friends of a downright nature may regard this weakness as an advantage, and I myself certainly enjoyed giving the lectures. Now they are published, I notice their weak points and will not grumble at any reviewer who brings them to my attention.

When I finally yielded to the pressure put upon me by the representatives of the *Verlag Zollikon*, I did so thinking that what I had produced might in this looser form serve to explain things which I had elsewhere expressed more strictly and compactly but, for that very reason perhaps, less noticeably and less accessibly for all. Others, again, may possibly read the little book not without pleasure, because, although it does not have too many topical references, it smacks of a document of our time, which has once more become a time 'between the times'—and that not only in Germany. Lastly I said to myself that the Christian Confession not only can stand, it even demands, interpretation in such a key and tempo as you have here.

If I were to dedicate the book to anyone, I would dedicate it to my Bonn students and audience of summer, 1946, with whom I certainly had a grand time with these lectures.

BASEL.
February, 1947.

I

THE TASK

Dogmatics is the science in which the Church, in accordance with the state of its knowledge at different times, takes account of the content of its proclamation critically, that is, by the standard of Holy Scripture and under the guidance of its Confessions.

DOGMATICS is a science. What science really is has already been pondered, discussed and written about infinitely often and at all periods. We cannot develop this discussion even allusively here. I offer you a concept of science which is at any rate discussible and may serve as the basis for our expositions. I propose that by science we understand an attempt at comprehension and exposition, at investigation and instruction, which is related to a definite object and sphere of activity. No act of man can claim to be more than an attempt, not even science. By describing it as an attempt, we are simply stating its nature as preliminary and limited. Wherever science is taken in practice completely seriously, we are under no illusion that anything man can do can ever be an undertaking of supreme wisdom and final art, that there exists an absolute science, one that as it were has fallen from Heaven. Even Christian dogmatics is an attempt—an attempt to understand and an attempt to expound, an attempt to see, to hear and to state definite facts, to survey and co-ordinate these facts, to present them in the form of a doctrine. In every science an object is involved and a sphere of activity. In no science is it a matter of pure theory or pure practice; on the one hand, theory comes in, but also, on the other hand, practice guided by this theory. So by dogmatics, too, we understand this twofold activity of investigation and doctrine in relation to an object and a sphere of activity.

The subject of dogmatics is the Christian Church. The subject of a science can only be one in which the object and sphere of activity in question are present and familiar. Therefore it is no limitation and no vilification of the concept of dogmatics as a science to say that the subject of this science is the Church. It is the place, the community, charged with the object and the

activity with which dogmatics is concerned—namely, the proclamation of the Gospel. By calling the Church the subject of
dogmatics we mean that where dogmatics is pursued, whether by
pupil or by teacher, we find ourselves in the sphere of the Church.
The man who seeks to occupy himself with dogmatics and
deliberately puts himself outside the Church would have to reckon
with the fact that for him the object of dogmatics would be alien,
and should not be surprised if after the first steps he could not find
his bearings, or even did damage. Even in dogmatics familiarity
with the subject must be there, and this really means familiarity
with the life of the Church. This, of course, cannot mean that in
dogmatics one would have to deal with what had been said in
ancient or modern times by a Church authority, so that we should
merely be repeating what it had prescribed. Not even Roman
Catholic dogmatics has so interpreted its task. By calling the
Church the subject of dogmatics, our only thought is that whoever
is occupied with this science, whether as pupil or as teacher, must
take his stand in responsibility upon the basis of the Christian
Church and its work. That is the *conditio sine qua non*. But please
note that this involves a free participation in the Church's life;
it involves the responsibility which the Christian has to shoulder
in this matter also.

In the science of dogmatics the Church draws up its reckoning
in accordance with the state of its knowledge at different times.
It might be said that this is quite obvious, given the premised
concept of science. But it is not so automatically obvious, according to certain ideas about dogmatics which many have in their
heads. I repeat that dogmatics is not a thing which has fallen from
Heaven to earth. And if someone were to say that it would be
wonderful if there were such an absolute dogmatics fallen from
Heaven, the only possible answer would be: 'Yes, if we were
angels.' But since by God's will we are not, it will be good for us to
have just a human and earthly dogmatics. The Christian Church
does not exist in Heaven, but on earth and in time. And although
it is a gift of God, He has set it right amid earthly and human
circumstances, and to that fact corresponds absolutely everything
that happens in the Church. The Christian Church lives on earth
and it lives in history, with the lofty good entrusted to it by God.
In the possession and administration of this lofty good it passes on
its way through history, in strength and in weakness, in faithfulness and in unfaithfulness, in obedience and in disobedience, in

understanding and in misunderstanding of what is said to it. Amid the history unfolded upon earth, for example, that of nature and civilisation, of morals and religion, of art and science, of society and the State, there is also a history of the Church. It too is a human, earthly history; and so it is not quite indefensible for Goethe to say of it that in all periods it has been a hotch-potch of error and power. If we Christians are sincere, we have to concede that this holds no less of Church history than of world history. That being so, we have cause to speak modestly and humbly of what the Church is capable of, and therefore also of the Church work that we are doing here—namely, dogmatics. Dogmatics will always be able to fulfil its task only in accordance with the state of the Church at different times. It is because the Church is conscious of its limitations that it owes a reckoning and a responsibility to the good it has to administer and to cherish, and to the good One who has entrusted this good to it. It will never be able to do this perfectly; Christian dogmatics will always be a thinking, an investigation and an exposition which are relative and liable to error. Even dogmatics with the best knowledge and conscience can do no more than question after the better, and never forget that we are succeeded by other, later men; and he who is faithful in this task will hope that those other, later men may think and say better and more profoundly what we were endeavouring to think and to say. With quiet sobriety and sober quietness, we shall do our work in this way. We must use our knowledge as it has been given to us to-day. No more can be required of us than is given to us. And like a servant who is faithful in little, we must not be sorrowful about such little. More than this faithfulness is not required of us.

As a science dogmatics takes account of the content of proclamation in the Christian Church. There would be no dogmatics and there would perhaps be no theology at all, unless the Church's task consisted centrally in the proclamation of the Gospel in witness to the Word spoken by God. This task, which rises up again and again, this problem put to the Church from the beginning, the problem of instruction, doctrine, witness, proclamation, really stands as the question, not just for parsons and theologians, but again and again before the Church as a whole: What as Christians do we really have to say? For undoubtedly the Church should be the place where a word reverberates right into the world. Since the Church's task is to proclaim the Word spoken by God, which is still at the same time a human work, theology and what we to-day—practically since the seventeenth century—term dogmatics have been necessary from the beginning. In theology there is the question as to the source or provenance of the Word; and the answer to this first question will have to be given again and again in that discipline which we call exegesis. But on the other hand there also arises the question, *how?*—that is, the question about the shape and form of the proclamation enjoined upon the Church; and there we find ourselves in the field of what is termed practical theology. Exactly halfway between exegesis and practical theology stands dogmatics, or, more comprehensively expressed, systematic theology. In dogmatics we do not ask whence Church proclamation comes and what its form is. In dogmatics our question is: *What* are we to think and say? Of course, that comes after we have learned from Scripture where we have to draw this 'what' from, and keeping in view the fact that we have to say something not just theoretically, but have to call something out to the world. Precisely from this dogmatic standpoint it must be clear that the whole of theology is on the one hand really not a mere historicism, that the history is valid, the history which penetrates into the present day, *hic et nunc*. Of course, on the other hand, preaching must not degenerate into a mere technique. In fact, in our time of need to-day the question is more insistent than ever, what the content of Christian proclamation ought to be. I should like you to pause by this 'what' for a little. It is for the sake of this question that we study not only exegesis and practical theology, but dogmatics. In order not to exclude Church history, I might just add that its task is encyclopædic. Its special honour is to be, as it were, everywhere in the scheme, and so to have its place in Christian instruction as well.

Dogmatics is a critical science. So it cannot be held, as is sometimes thought, that it is a matter of stating certain old or even new propositions that one can take home in black and white. On the contrary, if there exists a critical science at all, which is constantly having to begin at the beginning, dogmatics is that science. Outwardly, of course, dogmatics arises from the fact that the Church's proclamation is in danger of going astray. Dogmatics is the testing of Church doctrine and proclamation, not an arbitrary testing from a freely chosen standpoint, but from the standpoint of the Church which in this case is the solely relevant standpoint. The concrete significance of this is that dogmatics measures the Church's proclamation by the standard of the Holy Scriptures, of the Old and New Testaments. Holy Scripture is the document of the basis, of the innermost life of the Church, the document of the manifestation of the Word of God in the person of Jesus Christ. We have no other document for this living basis of the Church; and where the Church is alive, it will always be having to re-assess itself by this standard. We cannot pursue dogmatics without this standard being kept in sight. We must always be putting the question, 'What is the evidence?' Not the evidence of my thoughts, or my heart, but the evidence of the apostles and prophets, as the evidence of God's self-evidence. Should a dogmatics lose sight of this standard, it would be an irrelevant dogmatics.

The second point we mentioned in the opening statement referred to 'the guidance of its Confessions'. Holy Scripture and the Confessions do not stand on the same level. We do not have to respect the Bible and tradition with the like reverence and love, not even tradition in its most dignified manifestations. No Confession of the Reformation or of our own day can claim the respect of the Church in the same degree that Scripture in its uniqueness deserves it. But that does not at all alter the fact that in the Church the witness of the Fathers is listened to and respected. In it we are not listening to God's Word, as we do in Jeremiah or St. Paul. But it still possesses for us a lofty and important significance; and obedient to the command to 'honour father and mother', we shall not refuse, in the task of preaching, or in the scientific task of dogmatics, to respect what our fathers have said. If Holy Scripture has binding authority, we cannot say the same of the Confessions. Yet there is still a non-binding authority, which must be taken seriously. As our natural parents do not stand before us like God but nevertheless are in authority over us, so here too we have to do with a relative authority. Using this standard and critical in this sense, dogmatics approaches its task of giving an account of the content of proclamation, of the relation between actual proclamation and what, as truly reproducing what was said to the Church, ought to be valid in the Church. To that which ought to be valid in the Church as reproducing the Word of God, we give the name of 'dogma'. The Church asks and must continually ask itself to what extent that which takes place in Church proclamation corresponds to dogma. The purpose is simply to improve the form of Church proclamation. The correction, the deepening, the increasing precision of what is taught in our Church can only be God's own work although not apart from man's effort. One part of this effort is dogmatics.

Our intention here is to carry on with dogmatics in outline; in this short summer term we are only concerned with a sketch. We wish to pursue dogmatics in connexion with—that is, under the guidance of—a classical text, the Apostles' Creed.

There is no utterly necessary, no absolutely prescribed method of Christian dogmatics—that is, the road we have to take in detail is left to the best knowledge and conscience of the man engaged in this matter. Certainly in the course of the centuries a procedure has been built up which has, so to speak, become usual, the procedure which generally follows the outline of Christian thought upon God—namely God the Father, the Son, and the Holy Spirit. But in all details innumerable ways have been traversed and are possible. We choose the simplest way of all, the Confession of the Church, familiar to you all, as recited in our services Sunday by Sunday. It is not the historical question that engages us. It is well known to you that 'Apostles' in the Confession of faith should be put within inverted commas. It was not the apostles who uttered this Confession. In its present wording, it probably derives from the third century and goes back to an original form confessed and acknowledged in the congregation of Rome. It next spread as the basic form in the Christian Church, so that we may justly take it as a classical form.

2

FAITH AS TRUST

THE Confession begins with the significant words, 'I believe'.
This indicates that we link up all that is to be said as fundamental to our task with this simple introduction to the Confession.
We start with three leading propositions, which describe the
nature of faith.

> *Christian faith is the gift of the meeting in which men become free
> to hear the word of grace which God has spoken in Jesus Christ in
> such a way that, in spite of all that contradicts it, they may once
> for all, exclusively and entirely, hold to His promise and guidance.*

Christian faith, Church proclamation, which, as we stated,
is the cause and basic reason for dogmatics, deals—well, what does
it deal with? With the fact that Christians believe? And the way
in which Christians believe? Actually, this fact, the subjective
form of faith, the *fides qua creditur*, cannot possibly be quite excluded
from proclamation. Where the gospel is proclaimed, there too of
necessity the fact will be proclaimed along with it that there are
men who have heard and accepted the gospel. But the fact that
we believe can only be, *a priori*, a secondary matter, becoming
small and unimportant in face of the outstanding and real thing
involved in the Christian proclamation—*what* the Christian
believes, that is, what must be confirmed as the content and object
of his faith, and *what* we have to preach, that is, the object with
which the Apostles' Creed deals: I believe in God, the Father, the
Son and the Holy Spirit. More popularly the Confession is called
the 'Belief'; and by this 'Belief' we are at the very least to realise
the fact that we believe. In Christian faith we are concerned quite
decisively with a meeting. 'I believe in'—so the Confession says;
and everything depends on this 'in', this *eis*, this *in* (Latin). The
Creed explains this 'in', this object of faith, by which our subjective faith lives. It is noteworthy that, apart from this first
expression 'I believe', the Confession is silent upon the subjective
fact of faith. Nor was it a good time when this relationship was
reversed, when Christians grew eloquent over their action, over
the uplift and emotion of the experience of this thing, which took

place in man, and when they became speechless as to *what* we may believe. By the silence of the Confession on the subjective side, by its speaking only of the objective Creed, it also speaks at its best, deepest and completest about what happens to us men, about what we may be, do, and experience. Here too it is true that whoso would keep his life shall lose it; but whoso shall lose it for My sake shall gain his life. Whoso means to rescue and preserve the subjective element shall lose it; but whoso gives it up for the sake of the objective, shall save it. I believe—of course! It is my, it is a human, experience and action, that is, a human form of existence.

But this 'I believe' is consummated in a meeting with One who is not man, but God, the Father, Son, and Holy Spirit, and by my believing I see myself completely filled and determined by this object of my faith. And what interests me is not myself with my faith, but He in whom I believe. And then I learn that by thinking of Him and looking to Him, my interests are also best provided for. I believe in, *credo in*, means that I am not alone. In our glory and in our misery we men are not alone. God comes to meet us and as our Lord and Master He comes to our aid. We live and act and suffer, in good and in bad days, in our perversity and in our rightness, in this confrontation with God. I am not alone, but God meets me; one way or other, I am in all circumstances in company with Him. That is, I believe in God, the Father, the Son, and the Holy Spirit. This meeting with God is the meeting with the word of grace which He has spoken in Jesus Christ. Faith speaks of God, the Father, the Son and the Holy Spirit, as Him who meets us, as the object of faith, and says of this God that He is one in Himself, has become single in Himself for us and has become single once more in the eternal decree, explicated in time, of His free, unowed, unconditional love for man, for all men, in the counsel of His grace. God is gracious to us— this is what the Confession of the Father, Son and Holy Spirit, says. This includes the fact that of ourselves we cannot achieve, have not achieved, and shall not achieve a togetherness with Him; that we have not deserved that He should be our God, have no power of disposal and no rights over Him, but that with unowed kindness, in the freedom of His majesty, He resolved of His own self to be man's God, our God. He *tells* us that this is so. God's telling us, 'I am gracious to you', is the Word of God, the central concept of all Christian thinking. The Word of God is the word of His grace. And if you ask me where we hear this Word of God, I can only point to Himself, who enables us to hear it, and reply with the mighty centre of the Confession, with the second article, that the Word of God's grace in which He meets us is called Jesus Christ, the Son of God and Son of man, true God and true Man, Immanuel, God with us in this One. Christian faith is the meeting with this 'Immanuel', the meeting with Jesus Christ and in Him with the living Word of God. In calling Holy Scripture the Word of God (and we so call it, because it is so), we mean by it Holy Scripture as the witness of the prophets and the apostles to this one Word of God, to Jesus, the man out of Israel, who is God's Christ, our Lord and King in eternity. And in confessing this, in venturing to call the Church's proclamation God's Word, we must be understood to mean the proclamation of Jesus Christ, of Him who is true God and true Man for our good. In Him God meets us. And when we say, I believe *in* God, the concrete meaning is that I believe in the Lord Jesus Christ.

I have described this meeting as a gift. It is a meeting in which men become free to hear God's Word. The gift and the becoming free belong to each other. The gift is the gift of a freedom, of the great freedom in which all other freedoms are included. I really wish I might succeed, this term, in restoring to your favour this much misused and yet most noble word 'freedom', starting from this centre or core outwards. Freedom is God's great gift, the gift of meeting with Him. Why a gift, and why a gift of freedom? What it means is that this meeting of which the Creed speaks does not take place in vain. It rests not upon a human possibility and human initiative, nor on the fact that we men bear in us a capacity to meet God, to hear His Word. Were we to reckon up for ourselves what we men are capable of, we should strive in vain to discover anything which might be termed a disposition towards the Word of God. Without any possibility on our side God's great possibility comes into view, making possible what is impossible from our side. It is God's gift, God's free gift, not prepared for by anything on our side, *if* we meet Him and in meeting with Him hear His Word. The Creed of the Father, Son and Holy Spirit speaks in all three articles of a nature and work absolutely new to us men, inaccessible and inconceivable to us. And as this nature and work of God the Father, the Son and the Holy Spirit is His free grace towards us, it is grace all over again if our eyes and ears are opened to this grace. As it is the mystery of God of which the Creed speaks, we are set in its midst when it is disclosed to us, when we become free to know it and to live in it. 'I believe that not of my own reason and power do I believe in my Lord or am able to come to Him', says Luther. I believe; so then, it is itself a recognition of faith, to recognise that God is to be known only through God Himself. And if we can repeat this in faith, it means that I give praise and thanks for the fact that God the Father, the Son and the Holy Spirit is what He is and does what He does, and has disclosed and revealed Himself to me, has determined Himself for me and me for Himself. I give praise and thanks for the fact that I am elect, that I am called, that my Lord has made me free for Himself. In that confidence I believe. That which I do in believing is the only thing left me, to which I have been invited, to which I have been made free by Him who can do what I can neither begin nor accomplish of myself. I make use of the gift in which God has given me Himself. I breathe, and now I breathe joyfully and freely in the freedom which I have not taken to myself, which I have not sought nor found by myself, but in which God has come to me and adopted me. It is a matter of freedom to hear the word of grace in such a way that man may hold to this word. To hold to a word means that this word is credible to me. The world is full of words, and nowadays we realise what it means when an inflation of words is reached—that is, when all old words lose their value, when they cease to have any currency. Where there is faith in the gospel, there the Word has found confidence, there the Word has so let itself be heard that the hearer cannot withdraw from it. There the Word has acquired its meaning as the Word and been established.

This remarkable Word in which faith believes is the Word of God, Jesus Christ, in whom God has spoken His Word to man once for all. So faith means trust. Trust is the act in which a man may rely on the faithfulness of Another, that His promise holds and that what He demands He demands of necessity. 'I believe' means 'I trust'. No more must I dream of trusting in myself, I no longer require to justify myself, to excuse myself, to attempt to save and preserve myself. This most profound effort of man to trust to himself, to see himself as in the right, has become pointless. I believe—not in myself—I believe in God the Father, the Son and the Holy Ghost. So also trust in any sort of authorities, who might offer themselves to me as trustworthy, as an anchor which I ought

to hold on to, has become frail and superfluous. Trust in any sort
of gods has become frail and superfluous. These are the gods set
up, honoured and worshipped by men in ancient and recent times:
the authorities on whom man relies, no matter whether they have
the form of ideas or of any sort of powers of destiny, no matter
what they are called. Faith delivers us from trust in such gods,
and therefore also from fear of them, from the disillusionments
which they inevitably prepare for us again and again. We are
given freedom to trust in Him who deserves our trust: freedom by
holding to Him who in distinction from all other authorities is
and will remain faithful. We ourselves shall never be true to ourselves. Our human path is, as such, a path from one disloyalty
to another; and it is the same with the ways of the gods of this
world. They do not keep what they promise. So with them there
is never any real peace and clarity. In God alone is there faithfulness, and faith is the trust that we may hold to Him, to His
promise and to His guidance. To hold to God is to rely on the
fact that God is there for me, and to live in this certainty. This is
the promise God gives us: I am there for you. But this promise at
once means guidance too. I am not left to my waywardness and
my own ideas; but I have His commandment, to which I may
hold in everything, in my entire earthly existence. The Creed is
always at the same time the gospel, God's glad tidings to man,
the message of Immanuel, God with us, to us; and as such it is
necessarily also the law. Gospel and law are not to be separated;
they are one, in such a way that the gospel is the primary thing,
that the glad tidings are first in the field and, as such, include the
law. Because God is for us, we may also be for Him. Because He
has given Himself to us, we may also in gratitude give Him the
trifle which we have to give. To hold to God thus always means
that we receive everything wholly from God and so are wholly
active for Him.

And this 'in spite of all that contradicts it, once for all, exclusively and entirely'. In these four categories faith is once more
described as trust. When we say that faith involves *in spite of*, once
for all, exclusively and entirely, we are to hold to the fact that in
faith is involved a 'may', not a 'must'. The moment the thing
becomes an ideal instance we have again dropped out of the glory
of faith. The glory of faith does not consist in our being challenged
to do something, in having something laid upon us which is
beyond our strength. Faith is rather a freedom, a permission. It is

permitted to be so—that the believer in God's Word may hold on to this Word in everything, in spite of all that contradicts it. It is so: we never believe 'on account of', never 'because of'; we awake to faith in spite of everything. Think of the men in the Bible. They did not come to faith by reason of any kind of proofs, but one day they were so placed that they might believe and then had to believe in spite of everything. God is hidden from us outside His Word. But He is manifest to us in Jesus Christ. If we look past Him, we must not be surprised if we fail to find God and experience errors and disillusionments, if the world seems dark to us. When we believe, we must believe in spite of God's hiddenness. This hiddenness of God necessarily reminds us of our human limitation. We do not believe out of our personal reason and power. Anyone who really believes knows that. The greatest hindrance to faith is again and again just the pride and anxiety of our human hearts. We would rather not live by grace. Something within us energetically rebels against it. We do not wish to receive grace; at best we prefer to give ourselves grace. This swing to and fro between pride and anxiety is man's life. Faith bursts through them both. Of his own strength a man cannot do it. We cannot deliver ourselves from pride and anxiety about life; but there will always be a movement of defiance, not last against ourselves. If we summarise all that opposes as the power of contradiction, one has an inkling of what Scripture means by the devil. 'Has God really said . . .?' Is God's Word true? If one believes, one will snap one's fingers at the devil. But it is no human act of heroism to believe. Beware of wanting to make a hero of Luther. Luther himself never felt like one; but he realised that if we may defy, it is really a 'may', a permission, a freedom which we can only receive in deepest humility.

And faith is concerned with a decision *once for all*. Faith is not an opinion replaceable by another opinion. A temporary believer does not know what faith is. Faith means a final relationship. Faith is concerned with God, with what He has done for us once for all. That does not exclude the fact that there are fluctuations in faith. But seen with regard to its object, faith is a final thing. A man who believes once believes once for all. Don't be afraid; regard even that as an invitation. One may, of course, be confused and one may doubt; but whoever once believes has something like a *character indelibilis*. He may take comfort of the fact that he is being upheld. Everyone who has to contend with unbelief should be advised that he ought not to take his own unbelief too seriously. Only faith is to be taken seriously; and if we have faith as a grain of mustard seed, that suffices for the devil to have lost his game.

And, thirdly, faith is concerned with our holding to God *exclusively*, because God is the One who is faithful. There is also human faithfulness, a faithfulness of God, which may look at us out of His creatures and rejoice and strengthen us; but where such faithfulness exists, its basis will always be the faithfulness of God. To believe is the freedom to trust in Him quite alone, *sola gratia* and *sola fide*. This signifies not an impoverishment of human life, but rather that the riches of God are assigned to us.

And, in conclusion, we may hold *entirely* to God's Word. Faith is not concerned with a special realm, that of religion, say, but with real life in its totality, the outward as well as the inward questions, that which is bodily as well as that which is spiritual, the brightness as well as the gloom in our life. Faith is concerned with our being permitted to rely on God as regards ourselves and also as regards what moves us on behalf of others, of the whole of humanity; it is concerned with the whole of living and the whole of dying. The freedom to have this trust (understood in this comprehensive way) is faith.

3

FAITH AS KNOWLEDGE

Christian faith is the illumination of the reason in which men become free to live in the truth of Jesus Christ and thereby to become sure also of the meaning of their own existence and of the ground and goal of all that happens.

POSSIBLY you may be struck by the emergence of the concept of *reason*. I use it deliberately. The saying, 'Despise only reason and science, man's supremest power of all', was uttered not by a prophet, but by Goethe's Mephisto. Christendom and the theological world were always ill-advised in thinking it their duty for some reason or other, either of enthusiasm or of theological conception, to betake themselves to the camp of an opposition to reason. Over the Christian Church, as the essence of revelation and of the work of God which constitutes its basis, stands the Word: 'The Word was made flesh.' The Logos became man. Church proclamation is language, and language not of an accidental, arbitrary, chaotic and incomprehensible kind, but language which comes forward with the claim to be true and to uphold itself as the truth against the lie. Do not let us be forced from the clarity of this position. In the Word which the Church has to proclaim the truth is involved, not in a provisional, secondary sense, but in the primary sense of the Word itself—the Logos is involved, and is demonstrated and revealed in the human reason, the human *nous*, as the Logos, that is, as meaning, as truth to be learned. In the word of Christian proclamation we are concerned with *ratio*, reason, in which human *ratio* may also be reflected and reproduced. Church proclamation, theology, is no talk or babbling; it is not propaganda unable to withstand the claim, Is it then true as well, this that is said? Is it really so? You have probably also suffered from a certain kind of preaching and edifying talk, from which it becomes only too clear that there is talking going on, emphatic talk with a plenteous display of rhetoric, which does not however stand up to this simple question as to the truth of what is said. The Creed of Christian faith rests upon knowledge. And where the Creed is uttered and confessed knowledge should be, is meant to be, created. Christian faith is not irrational, not anti-rational, not supra-national, but rational in the proper sense. The Church which utters the Creed, which comes forward with the tremendous claim to preach and to proclaim the glad tidings, derives from the fact that it has apprehended something—*Vernunft* comes from *vernehmen*—and it wishes to let what it has apprehended be apprehended again. These were always unpropitious periods in the Christian Church, when Christian histories of dogmatics and theology separated *gnosis* and *pistis*. *Pistis* rightly understood is *gnosis*; rightly understood the act of faith is also an act of knowledge. Faith means knowledge.

But once this is established, it must also be said that Christian faith is concerned with an illumination of the reason. Christian faith has to do with the object, with God the Father, the Son, and the Holy Spirit, of which the Creed speaks. Of course it is of the nature and being of this object, of God the Father, the Son, and the Holy Spirit, that He cannot be known by the powers of human knowledge, but is apprehensible and apprehended solely because of His own freedom, decision and action. What man can know by his own power according to the measure of his natural powers, his understanding, his feeling, will be at most something like a supreme being, an absolute nature, the idea of an utterly free power, of a being towering over everything. This absolute and supreme being, the ultimate and most profound, this 'thing in itself', has nothing to do with God. It is part of the intuitions and marginal possibilities of man's thinking, man's contrivance. Man is able to think this being; but he has not thereby thought God. God is thought and known when in His own freedom God makes Himself apprehensible. We shall have to speak later about God, His being and His nature, but we must now say that God is always the One who has made Himself known to man in His own revelation, and not the one man thinks out for himself and describes as God. There is a perfectly clear division there already, epistemologically, between the true God and the false gods. Knowledge of God is not a possibility which is open for discussion. God is the essence of all reality, of that reality which reveals itself to us. Knowledge of God takes place where there is actual experience that God speaks, that He so represents Himself to man that he cannot fail to see and hear

Him, where, in a situation which he has not brought about, in which he becomes incomprehensible to himself, man sees himself faced with the fact that he lives with God and God with him, because so it has pleased God. Knowledge of God takes place where divine revelation takes place, illumination of man by God, transmission of human knowledge, instruction of man by this incomparable Teacher.

We started from the point that Christian faith is a meeting. Christian faith and knowledge of Christian faith take place at the point where the divine reason, the divine Logos, sets up His law in the region of man's understanding, to which law human, creaturely reason must accommodate itself. When that happens, man comes to knowledge; for when God sets up His law in man's thought, in his seeing and hearing and feeling, the revelation of the truth is also reached about man and his reason, the revelation of man is reached, who cannot bring about of himself what is brought about simply by God Himself.

Can God be known? Yes, God can be known, since it is actually true and real that He is knowable through Himself. When that happens, man becomes free, he becomes empowered, he becomes capable—a mystery to himself—of knowing God. Knowledge of God is a knowledge completely effected and determined from the side of its object, from the side of God. But for that very reason it is genuine knowledge; for that very reason it is in the deepest sense free knowledge. Of course it remains a relative knowledge, a knowledge imprisoned within the limits of the creaturely. Of course it is especially true here that we are carrying heavenly treasures in earthen vessels. Our concepts are not adequate to grasp this treasure. Precisely where this genuine knowledge of God takes place it will also be clear that there is no occasion for any pride. There always remains powerless man, creaturely reason with its limitations. But in this area of the creaturely, of the inadequate, it has pleased God to reveal Himself. And since man is foolish in this respect too, He will be wise; since man is petty, He will be great; since man is inadequate, God is adequate. 'Let my grace suffice for thee. For my strength is mighty in the weak' holds good also for the question of knowledge.

In the opening statement we said that Christian faith has to do with the illumination of the reason, in which men become free to live in the truth of Jesus Christ. For the understanding of Christian knowledge of faith it is essential to understand that the truth of Jesus Christ is living truth and the knowledge of it living knowledge. This does not mean that we are to revert once more to the idea that here knowledge is not basically involved at all. It is not that Christian faith is a dim sensation, an a-logical feeling, experiencing and learning. Faith is knowledge; it is related to God's Logos, and is therefore a thoroughly logical matter. The truth of Jesus Christ is also in the simplest sense a truth of facts. Its starting-point, the Resurrection of Jesus Christ from the dead, is a fact which occurred in space and time, as the New Testament describes it. The apostles were not satisfied to hold on to an inward fact; they spoke of what they saw and heard and what they touched with their hands. And the truth of Jesus Christ is also a matter of thoroughly clear and, in itself, ordered human thinking; free, precisely in its being bound. But—and the things must not be separated—what is involved is living truth. The concept of knowledge, of *scientia*, is insufficient to describe what Christian knowledge is. We must rather go back to what in the Old Testament is called wisdom, what the Greeks called *sophia* and the Latins *sapientia*, in order to grasp the knowledge of theology in its fullness. *Sapientia* is distinguished from the narrower concept of *scientia*, wisdom is distinguished from knowing, in that it not only contains knowledge in itself, but also that this concept speaks of a knowledge which is practical knowledge, embracing the entire existence of man. Wisdom is the knowledge by which we may actually and practically live; it is empiricism and it is the theory which is powerful in being directly practical, in being the knowledge which dominates our life, which is really a light upon our path. Not a light to wonder at and to observe, not a light to kindle all manner of fireworks at—not even the profoundest philosophical speculations—but the light on our road which may stand above our action and above our talk, the light on our healthy and on our sick days, in our poverty and in our wealth, the light which does not only lighten when we suppose ourselves to have moments of insight, but which accompanies us even into our folly, which is not quenched when all is quenched, when the goal of our life becomes visible in death. To live by this light, by this truth, is the meaning of Christian knowledge. Christian knowledge means living in the truth of Jesus Christ. In this light we live and move and have our being (Acts 17. 28) in order that we may be of Him, and through Him and unto Him, as it says in Romans 11. 36. So Christian knowledge, at its deepest, is one with what we termed

man's trust in God's Word. Never yield when they try to teach
you divisions and separations in this matter. There is no genuine
trust, no really tenable, victorious trust in God's Word which is
not founded in His truth; and on the other hand no knowledge,
no theology, no confessing and no Scripture truth which does
not at once possess the stamp of this living truth. The one
must always be measured and tested and confirmed by the
other.

And just because as Christians we may live in the truth of
Jesus Christ and therefore in the light of the knowledge of God
and therefore with an illumined reason, we shall also become sure
of the meaning of our own existence and of the ground and goal
of all that happens. Once more a quite tremendous extension of
the field of vision is indicated by this; to know this object in its
truth means in truth to know no more and no less than all things,
even man, oneself, the cosmos, and the world. The truth of Jesus
Christ is not one truth among others; it is *the* truth, the universal
truth that creates all truth as surely as it is the truth of God, the
prima veritas which is also the *ultima veritas*. For in Jesus Christ God
has created all things, He has created all of us. We exist not apart
from Him, but in Him, whether we are aware of it or not; and
the whole cosmos exists not apart from Him, but in Him, borne
by Him, the Almighty Word. To know Him is to know all. To be
touched and gripped by the Spirit in this realm means being led
into all truth. If a man believes and knows God, he can no longer
ask, What is the meaning of my life? But by believing he actually
lives the meaning of his life, the meaning of his creatureliness, of
his individuality, in the limits of his creatureliness and individuality and in the fallibility of his existence, in the sin in which he is
involved and of which daily and hourly he is guilty; yet he also
lives it with the aid which is daily and hourly imparted to him
through God's interceding for him, in spite of him and without
his deserving it. He recognises the task assigned to him in this
whole, and the hope vouchsafed to him in and with this task,
because of the grace by which he may live and the praise of the
glory promised him, by which he is even here and now secretly
surrounded in all lowliness. The believer confesses this meaning
of his existence. The Christian Creed speaks of God as the ground
and goal of all that exists. The ground and goal of the entire cosmos
means Jesus Christ. And the unheard-of thing may and must be
said, that where Christian faith exists, there also exists, through

God's being trusted, inmost familiarity with the ground and goal of all that happens, of all things; there man lives, in spite of all that is said to the contrary, in the peace that passeth all understanding, and which for that very reason is the light that lightens our understanding.

4

FAITH AS CONFESSION

Christian faith is the decision in which men have the freedom to be publicly responsible for their trust in God's Word and for their knowledge of the truth of Jesus Christ, in the language of the Church, but also in worldly attitudes and above all in their corresponding actions and conduct.

CHRISTIAN faith is a decision. This is where we have to begin, and wish to begin. Christian faith, to be sure, is an event in the mystery between God and man; the event of the freedom in which God acts towards this man, and of the freedom which God gives this man. But this does not exclude, but actually includes the fact that where there is faith in the sense of the Christian Creed, *history* is taking place, that there something is being undertaken, completed and carried out in time by man. Faith is God's mystery breaking forth; faith is God's freedom and man's freedom in action. Where nothing occurred—in time, of course, that is, occurred visibly and audibly—there would be no faith either. For Christian faith is faith in God, and when the Christian Confession names God the Father, the Son and the Holy Spirit, it is pointing to the fact that in His inner life and nature God is not dead, not passive, not inactive, but that God the Father, the Son and the Holy Spirit exist in an inner relationship and movement, which may very well be described as a story, as an event. God Himself is not suprahistorical, but historical. And this God has in Himself made a decree, an eternal decree, upon which everything rests of which the Confession of Faith speaks. Our fathers called it the decree of creation and of the covenant and of redemption. This decree of God was carried out in time, once for all, in the work and in the word of Jesus Christ, to which Article II of the Confession bears concrete testimony, 'who suffered under Pontius Pilate, was crucified, dead and buried. . . .' Faith is man's answer to this historical existence and nature and action of God. Faith has to do with the God who is in Himself historical and has fashioned a decree whose goal is history, and has set this history going and completed it. Christian

faith which was not itself history would not be Christian faith,
not faith in . . . Where there is Christian faith there arises
and grows an historical form, there arises among men, among
contemporaries and non-contemporaries, a *community*, a togetherness, a brotherhood. But by means of this community, we inevitably reach, at the point where faith is Christian, a human
proclamation and message as well, to the *world* outside this communion and brotherhood. A light is kindled there, which lightens
all them that are in the house. In other words, where Christian
faith exists, there God's congregation arises and lives in the world
for the world; there Israel gathers apart from the Gentiles of the
world; and there the Church gathers on its own behalf, the communion of saints. Yet not for its own purposes, but as the manifestation of the Servant of God, whom God has set there for all
men, as the Body of Christ. And this story happens—now we reach
the human work which answers to God's work and nature in the
election of His grace—in the answer of obedience. Faith is
obedience, not just a passive accommodation of oneself. Where
there is obedience, there is also choice on man's part; faith is
chosen instead of its opposite, unbelief, trust instead of distrust,
knowledge instead of ignorance. Faith means choosing between
faith and unbelief, wrong belief and superstition. Faith is the act
in which man relates himself to God as is appropriate to God. For
this work takes place in a stepping out of neutrality towards God,
out of any disavowal of obligation towards Him in our existence
and attitude, out of the private sphere, into resoluteness, responsibility and public life. Faith without this tendency to public life,
faith that avoids this difficulty, has become in itself unbelief,
wrong belief, superstition. For faith that believes in God the
Father, the Son and the Holy Spirit cannot refuse to become
public.

'Christian faith is the decision in which men have the freedom
. . .' said the opening sentence. In public responsibility, too,
there is a permission granted to men, an open door, and that
means a freedom. To freedom of trust and freedom of knowledge we must now add freedom of responsibility. Here one
freedom is inseparable from the other. If you merely want to
be free to trust God and think you can then renounce knowledge,
you would not in fact be trusting Him. And if you had all trust
and all knowledge and did not have the freedom to answer
publicly for your trust and your knowledge, you would have to

be told straight that all is not well with your trust and your knowledge! In accordance with what the Christian Church confesses of Him, God Himself is He who did not wish to remain hidden, who did not and does not wish to be God for Himself alone. He is the God who in His royal majesty emerges from the mystery, from the heights of His divine existence and comes down to the humble estate of the universe created by Him. God Himself is He who is revealed as God. He who believes in this God cannot wish to hide this God's gift, this God's love, this God's comfort and light, to hide his trust in His Word and His knowledge. The word and the work of the believer cannot possibly remain a neutral, uncommitted work and word. Where there is faith, God's *doxa, gloria*, His brightness is necessarily made known on earth. And where God's glory did not shine one way or another, however overcast and broken by our ways and our degeneration, there would be no faith; the comfort and the light we receive from God would not be accepted. God's glory is hallowed in the universe, and the Name of the Holy One hallowed on earth, where men may believe, where God's people, God's congregation assembles and goes into action. Where there is faith, man in his complete limitation and helplessness, in his utter abandonment and folly, possesses the freedom, the freedom royal in all humility, to let the light shine of the *doxa*, of the *gloria*, of the glory of God. More is not required of us; but that is required of us. This public responsibility of our trust in God's Word and of our knowledge of the truth of Jesus Christ is the general concept for what in the Christian sense is called confessing and confession.

There is public responsibility in the Church's language, but also in worldly attitudes and also and above all in the corresponding actions and conduct. In these three definitions of the concept of public responsibility, there are, if my diagnosis is correct, three forms of Christian confessing, inseparable from one another, not to be played off against one another, but necessarily to be thought of together; a confessing which, for its part, is an indispensable, basic form of Christian faith. The following expositions are therefore to be regarded as a synthesis.

1. In faith we have the freedom to be publicly responsible *in the language of the Church* for our trust and our knowledge. What does this mean? God's congregation possessed and at all times possesses its own language. Nothing can change this. For it has in history

its own special history, its own special road. It speaks, when it confesses, in relation to this special history. It stands in the quite special concrete historical context, which has at all times formed its language and will continue to form it. Therefore the language of faith, the language of public responsibility in which as Christians we are bound to speak, will inevitably be the language of the Bible, the Hebrew and the Greek Bible and the translations of them, and the language of Christian tradition, the language in the forms of the thoughts, concepts and ideas, in which in the course of centuries the Christian Church has gained and upheld and declared its knowledge. There is a specifically Church language. That is in order. Let us call it by the familiar name by saying that there is a 'language of Canaan'. And when the Christian confesses his faith, when we have to let the light that is kindled in us shine, no one can avoid speaking in this language. For this is how it is: if the things of Christian faith, if our trust in God and His Word is to be expressed precisely, so to speak in its essence—and time and again it is bitterly necessary for this to be done, so that things may be made clear—then it is inevitable that all undaunted the language of Canaan should sound forth. For certain lights and indications and heartening warnings can be uttered directly in this language alone. To anyone rather too sensitive in his desires and too tender about dealing with his soul—'I believe, but my faith is so deep and inward that I cannot bring myself to utter the words of the Bible, that it is difficult for me to pronounce God's name, let alone the name of Christ or the blood of Jesus Christ or the Holy Spirit'— to anyone who should speak in this strain, I would say: 'Dear friend, you may be a very spiritual man, but see to it that you are deemed worthy to be publicly responsible for your faith. And is your alleged shyness not shyness about emerging from your uncommitted private world? Ask yourself!' One thing is certain, that where the Christian Church does not venture to confess in its own language, it usually does not confess at all. Then it becomes the fellowship of the quiet, whereby it is much to be hoped that it does not become a community of dumb dogs. Where people believe, the urgent question arises whether they do not speak joyfully and gladly also, just as the Bible has spoken and as in ancient and more recent times the Church has spoken and must speak. Where faith in its freedom and joy is in the field, in this language too God's praise will be indeed uplifted and sung.

2. But this is not the end of the matter. More than this belongs to the complete concept of confessing. Let us be fully on our guard against the idea that confession is a matter of the faith which should be heard only in the 'area of the Church'. And that all that is to be done is to make this area visible and perhaps extend it a little into the world. The area of the Church stands in the world, as outwardly the Church stands in the village or in a city, beside the school, the cinema and the railway station. The Church's language cannot aim at being an end in itself. It must be made clear that the Church exists for the sake of the world, that the light is shining in the darkness. As Christ did not come to let Himself be ministered unto, so too it does not become Christians to exist in their faith, as though they existed for themselves. But that means that, in the course of this making public of trust and knowledge, faith necessarily stipulates definite worldly attitudes. Where confession is serious and clear, it must be fundamentally translatable into the speech of Mr. Everyman, the man and woman in the street, into the language of those who are not accustomed to reading Scripture and singing hymns, but who possess a quite different vocabulary and quite different spheres of interest. Such is the world into which Christ sent His disciples and in which all of us exist too. Not one of us is only a Christian; we are all also a bit of the world. And so we are necessarily also concerned with worldly attitudes, with translations of our responsibility into this realm. For the Confession of Faith claims to be fulfilled in its application to the life we all live, to the problems of our actual existence in the theoretical and practical questions of our everyday life. If our faith is real, it must encroach upon our life. The Christian Confession in its original Church form will always be exposed to the misunderstanding that the Christian regards the Creed as a matter of heart and conscience, but that here on earth and in the world other truths hold good. The world lives in this misunderstanding; it regards the whole of Christianity as a friendly 'magic', connected with the 'realm of religion', which is respected and which ought to be left untampered with; and so we get rid of the matter! But this misunderstanding might even come from within; a Christian might quite well wish to have this realm for himself and to guard faith like a sensitive plant. The relationship between the Church and the world has been widely understood as a question of a fixing of frontiers, whereby each secured itself behind its own frontier,

although from time to time it came to a skirmish. From the Church's standpoint, however, such a fixing of frontiers can never exhaust its task. By the very nature of the Christian Church there is only one task, to make the Confession heard in the sphere of the world as well. Not now repeated in the language of Canaan, but in the quite sober, quite unedifying language which is spoken 'out there'. There must be *translation*, for example, into the language of the newspaper. What we have to do is to say in the common language of the world the same thing as we say in the forms of Church language. The Christian need not be afraid of having to speak 'unedifyingly' as well. If a man cannot, let him consider whether he really knows how to speak edifyingly even in the Church. We know this language of the pulpit and the altar, which outside the area of the Church is as effectual as Chinese. Let us beware of remaining stuck where we are and refusing to advance to meet worldly attitudes. For instance, in 1933 in Germany there was plenty of serious, profound and living Christianity and confession—God be praised and thanked! But unfortunately this faith and confession of the German Church remained embedded in the language of the Church, and did not translate what was being excellently said in the language of the Church into the political attitude demanded at the time; in which it would have become clear that the Evangelical Church had to say 'No' to National Socialism, 'No' from its very roots. The confession of Christianity did not at the time become clear in *this* form. Think what would have happened, had the Evangelical Church at that time expressed its Church knowledge in the form of a worldly, political attitude. It was not capable of that and the results are open to the day. And as a second example there is, even to-day, serious, living Christianity. I am sure that the course of events has aroused in many hunger and thirst for the Word of God, and that a great hour has arrived for the Church. I hope that a space for the Church is not set up again and fortified, and the Christians gather among themselves. Theology must, of course, be pursued in all seriousness. But may we be confronted, and better than twelve years ago, with the fact that what has to happen in the Church must go out into the form of worldly attitudes. An evangelical Church which was to-day, say, prepared to keep silence on the question of guilt with regard to the events from which we have issued, which was unwilling to listen to this question which must be answered honestly for the sake of the future, would *a priori* condemn itself to unfruitfulness. A Church which was not clear on this point of having a duty to this nation in need, and not merely the task of giving Christian instruction in direct form, but which has the task of making this Christian instruction known in words which grapple with the problems of the day—a Church which was not filled with anxiety to discover this word, would *a priori* betake itself to a corner of the graveyard. May every individual Christian be clear that so long as his faith is a snail's shell, in which he feels comfortable, but which does not bother itself with the life of his people, so long, that is, as he lives in dualism, he has not yet really come to believe! This snail's shell is not a desirable residence. It is not good to be here. Man is a whole and can only exist as such a whole.

In conclusion, the last part of the introductory statement ends with 'the corresponding actions and attitudes'. I have deliberately distinguished this from the second point. What would it avail a man, if he should speak and confess in most powerful language, and had not love? Confession means a living confession. If you believe, you are challenged to pay in person, *payer de sa personne*. That is the crucial point.

5

GOD IN THE HIGHEST

God is He who according to Holy Scripture exists, lives, acts, makes Himself known to us in the work of His free love, resolved on and consummated in Jesus Christ: He, God alone.

THE Confession which we have made the basis of these lectures begins with the words, 'I believe in God'. In them we have pronounced the mighty word whose unfolding is the Christian Creed. God is the *Object* of the faith of which we have been speaking in the last lectures. God: that is, comprehensively regarded and expressed, the content of the proclamation of the Christian congregation. But now we are faced with the fact that this word 'God', that the concept of God, the idea of God seems to be a reality which is familiar in one way or another to all history of religion and philosophy. And before we go any further, we must stop a moment and ask ourselves how this word 'God', in the sense in which Christian faith utters it, is related to what has been so termed at all times and in all nations in the history of religion and philosophy. Let us be clear about what is usually meant by 'God' outside the Christian faith. When man speaks of God, of the divine nature, of the divine essence, or of God simply, then he means the object of the universally present and active longing, the object of man's homesickness and man's hope for a unity, a basis, a meaning to his existence, and the meaning of the world; he means thereby the existence and the nature of a Being who, whether in this or that connexion with the realities other than Himself, is to be regarded as the Supreme Being that determines and dominates all that exists. And if we glance at the history of human desire, human assertion about this Being, the first and strongest impression we receive is that of a human skill in invention, active on all sides and taking the most various routes; but also of human waywardness and human violence with this concept, this idea of God. Hence the picture of an infinite variety of possibilities, the picture of a great uncertainty, of great contradictions.

We must be clear that when we are speaking of God in the sense of Christian faith, He who is called God is not to be regarded as a continuation and enrichment of the concepts and ideas which usually constitute religious thought in general about God. In the sense of Christian faith, God is not to be found in the series of gods. He is not to be found in the pantheon of human piety and religious inventive skill. So it is not that there is in humanity something like a universal natural disposition, a general concept of the divine, which at some particular point involves the thing which we Christians call God and as such believe in and confess; so that Christian faith would be one among many, an instance within a general rule. A Christian Father once rightly said that *Deus non est in genere*, 'God is not a particular instance within a class'. When we Christians speak of 'God', we may and must be clear that this word signifies *a priori* the fundamentally Other, the fundamental deliverance from that whole world of man's seeking, conjecturing, illusion, imagining and speculating. It is not that on the long road of human seeking and longing for the divine a definite stopping-place has in the end been reached in the form of the Christian Confession. The God of the Christian Confession is, in distinction from all gods, not a found or invented God or one at last and at the end discovered by man; He is not a fulfilment, perhaps the last, supreme and best fulfilment, of what man was in course of seeking and finding. But we Christians speak of Him who completely takes the place of everything that elsewhere is usually called 'God', and therefore suppresses and excludes it all, and claims to be alone the truth. Where that is not realised, it is still not realised what is involved when the Christian Church confesses, 'I believe in God'. What is involved is man's meeting with the Reality which he has never of himself sought out or first of all discovered. 'What no eye hath seen nor ear heard, what hath not entered into the heart of any man, God hath given to those who love Him', is St. Paul's way of speaking of this matter. And there is no other way in which we can speak of it. God in the sense of the Christian Confession is and exists in a completely different way from that which is elsewhere called divine. And so His nature, His being is different from the nature and being of all alleged gods. We summarise all that is to be said of God, in the sense of the Christian Confession, in the words 'God in the Highest'. You all know where I take this idea from. It is in Luke 2. 14: 'Glory to God in the highest'; therefore our song is, 'Glory to God alone in the highest'. This 'in the highest', *in excelsis*, I shall now try to expound.

In view of what has been said so far, this 'in the highest' means quite simply that He is the One who stands *above* us and also above our highest and deepest feelings, strivings, intuitions, above the products, even the most sublime, of the human spirit. God in the highest means first of all—recalling what was said earlier—He who is in no way established in us, in no way corresponds to a human disposition and possibility, but who is in every sense established simply in Himself and is real in that way; and who is manifest and made manifest to us men, not because of our seeking and finding, feeling and thinking, but again and again only through Himself. It is this God in the highest who has turned as such to man, given Himself to man, made Himself knowable to him. God in the highest does not mean someone quite other, who has nothing to do with us, who does not concern us, who is eternally alien to us; God in the highest, in the sense of the Christian Confession, means He who from on high has condescended to us, has come to us, has become ours. God in the highest is the God who shows Himself to be the real God, and so the One who is in no way in our control and who none the less and just because of that has taken us to Himself. God is He who alone deserves to be called God, as distinct from all gods, different from all that exists otherwise, and yet the One who has united Himself to us. If we say with the Christian Confession, 'I believe in God' or 'I believe on God', we have to do with *this God*.

Let us attempt to describe more closely, in a few concrete sketches, what I have been outlining. I said that God is He who, according to Holy Scripture, exists, lives and acts, and makes Himself known. By this definition something fundamentally different is taking place from what would happen, if I should try and set before you conceptually arranged ideas of an infinite, supreme Being. In such a case I would be speculating. But I am not inviting you to speculate. I maintain that this is a radically wrong road which can never lead to God, but to a reality called so only in a false sense. God is He who is to be found in the book of the Old and New Testaments, which speaks of Him. And the Christian definition of God consists simply in the statement, 'He is spoken of there, so let us listen to what is said of Him there'. He who is to be seen and heard there is God. Note well: in the whole Bible of the Old and New Testaments not the slightest attempt is ever made to *prove* God. This attempt has always been made only outside the biblical view of God, and only where it has been forgotten with whom we have to do, when we speak of God. What sort of attempts were they, after all, where the attempt was made to *prove* a perfect Being alongside imperfect ones? Or from the existence of the world to prove its ultimate and supreme cause, God? Or from the alleged order of the world to prove the ordering Power? Or the moral proof of God from the face of man's conscience? I will not enter into these 'proofs' of God. I don't know whether you can at once see the humour and the fragility of these proofs. These proofs may avail for the alleged gods; if it were my task to make you acquainted with these allegedly supreme beings, I would occupy myself with the five famous proofs of God. In the Bible there is no such argumentation; the Bible speaks of God simply as of One who needs no proof. It speaks of a God who *proves Himself* on every hand: Here am I, and since I am and live and act it is superfluous that I should be proved. On the basis of this divine self-proof the prophets and apostles speak. In the Christian Church there can be no speaking about God in any other way. God has not the slightest need for our proofs. He who is called God in Holy Scripture is unsearchable—that is, He has not been discovered by any man. But when our talk is of Him and we speak of Him as about a familiar entity, who is more familiar and real than any other reality and who is nearer us than we are to ourselves, it is not because there may have been particularly pious people who were successful in investigating this Being, but because He who was hidden from us has disclosed Himself.

And it is part of this, that God is not only unprovable and unsearchable, but also *inconceivable*. No attempt is made in the Bible to define God—that is, to grasp God in our concepts. In the Bible God's name is named, not as philosophers do it, as the name of a timeless Being, surpassing the world, alien and supreme, but as the name of the living, acting, working Subject who makes Himself known. The Bible tells the story of God; it narrates His deeds and the history of this God in the highest, as it takes place on earth in the human sphere. The Bible proclaims the significance and the importance of this working and acting, this story of God, and in this way it proves God's existence, describes His being and His nature. Knowledge of God in the sense of Holy Scripture and the Confession is knowledge of His existence, His life, His action, His revelation in His work. And so the Bible is not a philosophical book, but a history book, the book of God's mighty acts, in which God becomes knowable by us.

Holy Scripture describes a work, and first the work of Creation. Alongside Himself God puts something else, something different from Himself—namely, the creature, without having need of it, in the power of His Almightiness, in His holy, overflowing love. Secondly, a covenant is set up between God and one of His creatures, between God and man. Once more an inconceivable fact: why precisely between God and *man*, of whom from the beginning it is narrated that he is unthankful to God, that he is a sinner? In spite of this sin, sovereignly overlooking it, reserving for Himself its amendment, God surrenders Himself. He lends Himself to become the God of a tiny, despised people in Asia Minor, Israel. He lends Himself to become a member of this people, a little child, and then to die. And thirdly—but the whole thing is one—there is the work of redemption, the unveiling of the purpose of God's free love for man and the world, the annihilation of all that would hinder this purpose; there is the revelation and the manifestation of the new heaven and the new earth. All this is a way, under the sign of the name of Jesus Christ, the man Jesus Christ, in whom God Himself has become visible and active on earth, who is at once the goal of the history of the nation Israel, and the beginning and starting-point of the Church, and at the same time the revelation of the redemption, of the completion, of the whole. The whole work of God lives and moves in this one Person. He who says God in the sense of Holy Scripture will necessarily have to say Jesus Christ over and over again.

This work of creation, of the covenant and of redemption is the reality in which God exists, lives and acts and makes Himself known. From this work we must make no abstractions, if we would know God's nature and existence. Here, in this work, God is the Person who expounds Himself, and is thus the subject of this work. It is the work of God's free love. We may venture to describe the reality which the work expounds, the nature and the essence of God, by these two concepts of freedom and love. But we must be careful, lest we tumble back again out of the concrete into the abstract, out of history into the realm of ideas. I would not say that God is freedom or that God is love—even though the second pronouncement is a biblical one. We do not know what love is and we do not know what freedom is; but *God* is love and *God* is freedom. What freedom is and what love is, we have to learn from Him. As predicate to this subject it may be said that He is the God of free love. In His work of creation, covenant and redemption, He proves Himself to be this God. It is there that we experience what love is, this desire of the other for his own sake, so that the one is no longer alone, but completely together with the other. This is love, this is God's *free* love. God is not lonely, not even without the world. He does not need the other and nevertheless He loves. This love cannot be understood apart from the majesty of His freedom. It is God's love, that He, the Father, loves the Son, who Himself is God. What in His work becomes visible is an uncovering of this mystery of His inner Being, where all is freedom and all is love.

And now perhaps the title of this lecture, 'God in the highest', becomes comprehensible. By being the Father, the Son and the Holy Ghost in His work in Jesus Christ, God is in the highest. He whose nature and essence consist, whose existence is proved, in His descending into the depths, He the Merciful, who gives Himself up for His creature to the utter depths of the existence of His creature—He is God in the highest. Not in spite of this, not in remarkable paradoxical opposition, but the highness of God consists in His thus descending. This is His exalted nature, this His free love. Anyone who wants to look up to some other height has not understood the utter otherness in God, he would still be in the tracks of the heathen, who look for God in an endlessness. But He is utterly other than we think our gods. It is He who calls Abraham and who led that wretched nation through the desert, who never swerves through the centuries-long disloyalty and disobedience of this nation, who causes Himself to be born in the stable at Bethlehem as a little child and who dies on Golgotha. He is the glorious Lord, He is divine. Do you understand what monotheism in Christian faith means? God knows, not the foolish delight in the number 'one'. It has nothing to do with the number 'one', but with this subject in His sheer uniqueness and otherness over against all others, different from all the ridiculous deities whom man invents. Once we have realised this, we can only laugh, and there is a laugh running through the Bible at these figures. Once the true God has been seen, the gods collapse into dust, and He remains the only One. 'I am the Lord thy God . . . thou shalt have no other gods before Me.' This 'thou shalt not' has the force of 'thou canst not'. He who calls himself god alongside Him becomes the mere shadow of man's extravagant longing, which has its ill results. And the Second Commandment also becomes quite clear then: 'Thou shalt not make unto thee any image nor any sort of likeness. Thou shalt not bow down to them nor worship them.' That too is not a sign of Israelite ways of thinking and there is no philosophical concept of invisibility in the background. But God has Himself done everything in order to present Himself. How should man make an image of Him after He has presented His likeness Himself? A well-intentioned business, this entire 'spectacle' of Christian art, well-intentioned but impotent, since God Himself has made His own image. Once a man has understood 'God in the highest', it becomes impossible for him to want any imagery in thought, or any other kind of imagery.

6

GOD THE FATHER

*The One God is by nature and in eternity the Father, the source
of His Son and, in union with Him, the source of the Holy Spirit.
In virtue of this way of being of His He is by grace the Father
of all men, whom He calls in time, in His Son and through His
Spirit, to be His children.*

THE One God, God in the highest, the Only God, is the
Father. In pronouncing this word, in saying Father along
with the first article of the Confession, we are straightway bound
to look ahead to the second, He is the Son, and to the third, He
is the Holy Spirit. It is the one God, of whom the three articles
of the Confession speak. These are not three Gods, a God split
and separated in Himself. The Trinity does not speak of three
Gods, but of the Trinity—that is how the Christian Church has
always understood it and could find it in no other form in Scripture—that speaks once again, and with all the more emphasis, of
the one, single God. This is no sort of theoretical business. But
everything depends on the fact that the content of the three
articles cannot be separated from each other, that in all that is
said in these three articles about God the Creator and God in His
action in Jesus Christ and in His operation as the Holy Spirit, it
is not a matter of three divine departments, with a 'Director' for
each. What is involved is the *one* work of the *One* God, but the one
work that is moved within itself. For God in whom we Christians
may believe is not a dead God, and He is not a lonely God. But
since He is the only God, He is in Himself, in His divine Majesty
in the highest, One, and yet not alone, and so His work in which
He meets us and in which we may know Him, is in itself a living
work, moved within itself; He is, in Himself by nature and in
eternity, and for us in time, *the One in three ways of being*. The
language of the early Church states that God is in three persons.
In the way in which the early Church understood the concept of
person, this concept is unassailable. For in Latin and in Greek
usage person meant exactly what I have just been describing as
'way of being'. But when we speak to-day of person, involuntarily

and almost irresistibly the idea arises of something rather like the way in which we men are persons. And actually this idea is as ill-suited as possible to describe what God the Father, the Son and the Holy Spirit is. Calvin once mockingly suggested that we should not imagine the triune God as all the artists have depicted Him, three manikins or *marmousets*. That is not the Trinity. But when the Christian Church speaks of the triune God, it means that God is not just in one way, but that He is the Father and the Son and the Holy Spirit. Three times the One and the Same, threefold, but above all triune, He, the Father, the Son and the Holy Spirit, in Himself and in the highest and in His revelation.

So above all we have to state that when God the 'Father' is called 'our Father', we are thereby saying something about God that is valid, that is true, and true, moreover, in the deepest depths of His nature, true unto all eternity. He is the Father. And exactly the same holds for the Son and for the Holy Spirit. Thus God's name of Father is not merely a surname which we men attach to God; so that the meaning would be that 'man thinks he knows something like fatherhood, like man's relationship to his father in the flesh, and now he transfers this relationship to God: the presupposition being that His nature is ultimately something quite different and has nothing to do with what we term fatherhood. That God is the Father holds true in view of His revelation, in view of us. But in Himself, by nature and in eternity, we do not know what He is. But He issues forth from this mystery of His and is then, and in this way, the Father for us.' But that is inadequate to describe the content with which in fact we are concerned here. When Holy Scripture and along with it the Confession of the Church calls God the Father, its meaning is that God is first of all Father. He is Father in Himself, by nature and in eternity, and then, following on that, for us as well, His creatures. It is therefore not that there is first of all human fatherhood and then a so-called divine Fatherhood, but just the reverse: true and proper fatherhood resides in God, and from this Fatherhood of God what we know as fatherhood among us men is derived. The divine Fatherhood is the primal source of all natural fatherhood. As is said in Ephesians, every fatherhood in heaven and on earth is of Him. We are thinking the truth, the first and proper truth, when we see God the Father in the ultimate, when we recognise Him as the Father, and may be called His children.

God the Father—in these words we are speaking of God's way
of being, as the source and origin of another divine way of being,
of a second one which is distinct from the first and which is yet
His way of being and so is identical with Him in His divinity.
God is God in such a way that He is the Father, the Father of
His Son, that he establishes Himself and through His own agency
is God a second time. Established by Himself, not created by
Himself—the Son is not created. But this relationship of Father
and Son does not yet exhaust the reality, the nature of God. It is
not that this establishing and being established of God threatens
the unity of God. It is the Father and the Son *together*, who clinch
the unity of God a third time in the Holy Spirit. God the Father
and God the Son are together the origin of the Holy Spirit:
Spiritus, qui procedit a Patre Filioque. It is this which the poor folk
in the Eastern Church have never quite understood, that the
Begetter and the Begotten are together the origin of the Holy
Spirit, and so the origin of their unity. The Holy Spirit has been
called the *vinculum caritatis*. Not *although* God is Father and Son,
but *because* God is Father and Son, unity exists. So God, as He who
establishes Himself, who exists through Himself, as God in His
deity, is in Himself different and yet in Himself alike. And for that
very reason He is not lonely in Himself. He does not need the
world. All richness of life, all fullness of action and community
exists in Himself, since He is the Triune. He is movement and He
is rest. Hence it can be plain to us that all that He is on our
behalf—that He is the Creator, that He has given us Himself in
Jesus Christ and that He has united us to Himself in the Holy
Spirit—is His free grace, the overflow of His fullness. Not owed to
us, but overflowing mercy! It is His will that what He is for Himself should be not only for Himself; but He wills to be for us also
the One He is in eternity. We have of ourselves no grip on this
truth, that God in the power of His eternal Fatherhood—of free
grace, not because it is His *métier*—wills to be also our Father.
Because He is what He is, His work also can only be His Fatherly
work. That God becomes the Creator of another, which in distinction from the Son is different from Him, that He wills to be
present for this other, means nothing else than that He gives us
a share in Himself. 'We become partakers of the divine nature'
(2 Pet. 1. 4). We say no more and no less when we call God our
Father. We may now call Him that which He names Himself
in His Son. Man as such is not God's child, but God's creature,·

factus and not *genitus*. This creature man is, so far as the eye reaches, in rebellion against God, is godless and nevertheless God's child. It is God's free work, His condescension and mercy, that we may be His children. We are that, we are because He is the Father and because He makes us so. We are His children *in His Son and through the Holy Spirit*, not on the ground of a direct relationship between us and God, but on the ground of the fact that God of Himself lets us participate in His nature, in His life and essence. It is God's good will and resolve that His relationship to us should be comprehended in His being, in His begetting of the Son; that we may be called His children in Him, in the Son through the Holy Spirit, through the same *vinculum caritatis* which unites the Father and the Son. Our calling is meant to be comprehended in this way of God's being as the Holy Spirit, and that, once more, is God's eternal decree. *You* are meant; for you it holds good and is to your good, what God is and does in His Son. And what is true in God's nature becomes true in time. So no more and no less than a repetition of the divine life, a repetition which we do not bring about and which we cannot take from ourselves, but which it is God's will to allow in the creaturely realm—that is, outside the Godhead. Glory to God in the highest! That is the first thing we utter, when we call God our Father. And 'peace on earth', because He is not the Father apart from the Son, and because both exist for us 'among men of good will'.

7

GOD ALMIGHTY

God's power differs from powerlessness, is superior to the other powers, is victoriously opposed to 'power in itself', in being the power of law, i.e. of His love activated and revealed in Jesus Christ and thus the content, the determination and the limit of everything possible, and the power over and in all that is real.

BY this concept 'Almighty' the Confession names an attribute of God, a perfection of Him who was previously called God the Father. The Confession knows only this one attribute. When attempts were later made to speak systematically about God and to describe His nature, men became more talkative. They spoke of God's aseity, His being grounded in. Himself; they spoke of God's infinity in space and time, and therefore of God's eternity. And men spoke on the other hand of God's holiness and righteousness, mercifulness and patience. We must be clear that whatever we say of God in such human concepts can never be more than an indication of Him; no such concept can really conceive the nature of God. God is inconceivable. What is called God's goodness and God's holiness cannot be determined by any view that we men have of goodness and holiness, but it is determined from what God is. He is the Lord, He is the truth. Only derivatively, only in a secondary sense can we venture to take His Word on our lips. In the Apostles' Creed there stands, in place of all possible descriptions of the nature of God, this one word, that He is Almighty, and significantly in connexion with the expression 'Father'. The one word explains the other; the Father is almightiness and almightiness is the Father.

'God is almighty' means in the first instance that He is might. And might means ability, possibility in view of a reality. Where reality is created, determined and preserved, there exists a possibility, lying at its basis. And now it is stated of God that He Himself has possibility, He has this ability which is the foundation of reality, its determinant and its support: he has almightiness, that is, He has *everything*, He is the basic measure of everything real and everything possible. There is no reality which does not rest upon Him as its possibility, no possibility, no basis of reality, which would limit Him or be a hindrance to Him. He is able to do what He wills. Thus God's power might also be described as God's *freedom*. God is simply free. The concepts of eternity, omnipresence, infinity are included in it. He is mighty over everything that is possible in space and in time; He is the measure and the basis of time and space; He has no limit. But all this has a very philosophic ring and with it we have by no means reached the meaning of almightiness as an attribute of God. There is much that is called might and would like to be called almightiness, which has nothing to do at all with the almightiness of God. We shall have to beware of constructing general concepts.

In the opening sentence limitations are drawn in three stages. God's power is different from powerlessness, it is superior to the other powers, and it is victoriously opposed to 'power in itself'.

God's power is different from all powerlessness. There is also a power of powerlessness, a possibility of the impossible, and that wholly or partially. But God is not wholly or partly powerlessness, but He is real power. He is not one who can do nothing, nor is He one who cannot do everything, but He is distinguished from all other powers by being able to do what He wills to do. Where powerlessness comes into question, there we have not to do with God. Where God is imagined in any sort of apartness, in great remoteness, He is not the one who is meant, but rather a being who is fundamentally weak. God has not the nature of a shadow, God is opposed to every powerlessness.

God is superior to all other powers. These other powers force themselves on our notice quite differently from God. They appear to be genuinely real. God is not in the series of these worldly powers, perhaps as the highest of them; but He is superior to all other powers, neither limited nor conditioned by them, but He is the Lord of all lords, the King of all kings. So that all these powers, which as such are indeed powers, are *a priori* laid at the feet of the power of God. In relation to Him they are not powers in rivalry with Him.

And the final stage, which is the most important one, because here most confusions menace us, is that God is not 'power in itself'. The essence of all power, namely ability, possibility, freedom as a neutral existence, absolute freedom, abstract ability, power in itself, is an intoxicating thought. Is God the essence of all sovereignty, simply *potentia*? He has often been understood as such, and it is natural to imagine this *potentia*, 'power in itself', as the divine, the most profound, truest and fairest, to admire, honour, worship and praise this power in itself as the mystery of existence. Perhaps you recall how, when Hitler used to speak about God, he called Him 'the Almighty'. But it is not 'the Almighty' who is God; we cannot understand from the standpoint of a supreme concept of power, who God is. And the man who calls 'the Almighty' God misses God in the most terrible way. For the 'Almighty' is bad, as 'power in itself' is bad. The 'Almighty' means Chaos, Evil, the Devil. We could not better discribe and define the Devil than by trying to think this idea of a self-based, free, sovereign ability. This intoxicating thought of power is chaos, the *tohu wabohu* which God in His creation has left behind Him, which He rejected when He created heaven and earth. That is the *opposite* of God; that is the danger by which the world that God created is continually threatened; it is the breaking-in, the offensive of this impossible possibility of free arbitrariness, which wishes to be just *potentia* in itself and to carry it out and as such to reign. Where 'power in itself' is honoured and worshipped, where 'power in itself' wishes to be the authority and wishes to impose law, we are dealing with the 'revolution of nihilism'. 'Power in itself' is *nihil*, and when 'power in itself' comes to the fore and wishes to dominate, then order is not created, but that is where revolution breaks out. 'Power in itself' is bad, is the end of all things. The power of God, real power, is opposed to 'power in itself'. It is also superior to it; and more, it is its opposite. God says *No* to this revolution of nihilism. And He is its victorious opposite; that is, by God's entering the field, that happens which happens when the sun breaks through the mist: then the power of this 'power in itself' falls and collapses. Then this concept is stripped bare in its abominableness, it loses the respect that is offered it. Then the evil spirits are compelled to flee. God and 'power in itself' are mutually exclusive. God is the essence of the possible; but 'power in itself' is the essence of the impossible.

To what extent is God's power opposed to 'power in itself'? To what extent is it superior to all powers and different from every powerlessness?

Holy Scripture never speaks of God's power, its manifestations and its victories, in separation from the concept of law: God's power is from the start the power of law. It is not mere *potentia* but *potestas*—that is, legitimate power based upon law.

What does 'law' mean? Looking back we must say that God's
power, and thus the power of the law, consists in the fact that it
is the omnipotence of God the Father. We have now to think of
what was described as the life of God the Father as Father of
His Son, the life of the God who is not lonely in Himself, but who
lives and reigns in eternity as the Father of His Son, who in His
inmost nature exists in this community. God's omnipotence as the
power of law is thus the power of the God who is in Himself
love. All that strives against this love, all solitude and solitary
self-assertion, is as such wrong and therefore not real power.
It is denied by God. But what God affirms is order, in the sense
in which order exists in God Himself, between Him and His Son
and the Holy Spirit. God's power is the power of order, the power
of the ordering of His love, which operates along lines of order
and leads to goals of order. God's power is holy, righteous, merciful, patient, kindly power. What distinguishes God's power from
impotence is that He is the triune God.

This power, God, is the power of His free love in Jesus Christ,
activated and revealed in Him. We must therefore look once more
upon God's work as the essence of all that is possible and real.
What in His grace God is and effects is the essence of all that is
called ability, freedom and possibility. God's power is not a
characterless power; and therefore all those childish questions,
whether God can bring it about that twice two equals five, and
the like, are pointless, because behind these questions stands an
abstract concept of 'ability'. A power which could lie would
not be a real power. It would be a powerlessness, a power of
zero, which believes it can assert and dispose of everything. It has
nothing to do with God and therefore nothing to do with real
power. God's power is genuine power and so it is over everything.
'I am God Almighty; walk before Me and be good.' From the
standpoint of this 'I' it is confirmed who Almighty God is and so
what omnipotence is. Or again, 'All power is given unto Me in
heaven and on earth'. To Him, Jesus Christ, it is given. In this
work of God His omnipotence becomes visible and alive as saving
and righteous power. In that way God is the content, the determination, the limit of all that is possible. And in that way He
is over all that is real as the transcendent God and He is in all
that is real as the immanent God—He, the Subject, who utters
this holy and good word and plies His holy and good work.

8

GOD THE CREATOR

In that God became man, it has also become manifest and worthy of belief that He does not wish to exist for Himself only and therefore to be alone. He does not grudge the world, distinct from Himself, its own reality, nature and freedom. His word is the power of its being as creation. He creates, sustains and rules it as the theatre of His glory—and in its midst, man also, as the witness of His glory.

I BELIEVE in God, the Father Almighty, Creator of heaven and earth. When we approach the truth which the Christian Church confesses in the word 'Creator', then everything depends on our realising that we find ourselves here as well confronted by the mystery of faith, in respect of which knowledge is real solely through God's revelation. The first article of faith in God the Father and His work is not a sort of 'forecourt' of the Gentiles, a realm in which Christians and Jews and Gentiles, believers and unbelievers are beside one another and to some extent stand together in the presence of a reality concerning which there might be some measure of agreement, in describing it as the work of God the Creator. What the meaning of God the Creator is and what is involved in the work of creation, is in itself not less hidden from us men than everything else that is contained in the Confession. We are not nearer to believing in God the Creator, than we are to believing that Jesus Christ was conceived by the Holy Spirit and born of the Virgin Mary. It is not the case that the truth about God the Creator is directly accessible to us and that only the truth of the second article needs a revelation. But in the same sense in both cases we are faced with the mystery of God and His work, and the approach to it can only be one and the same.

For the Confession does not speak of the world, or at all events it does so only incidentally, when it speaks of heaven and earth. It does not say, I believe in the created world, nor even, I believe in the work of creation. But it says, I believe in God the Creator. And everything that is said about creation depends absolutely upon this Subject. The same rule holds always, that all the predicates are determined by Him. This holds also for creation. Fundamentally what is involved here is the knowledge of the Creator; and after that and from that viewpoint His work must be understood.

It is of God the Creator we have to speak and therefore of His work as the *creation*, the making of heaven and earth. If we take this concept seriously, it must be at once clear that we are not confronted by a realm which in any sense may be accessible to human view or even to human thought. Natural science may be our occupation with its view of development; it may tell us the tale of the millions of years in which the cosmic process has gone on; but when could natural science have ever penetrated to the fact that there is one world which runs through this development? Continuation is quite a different thing from this sheer beginning, with which the concept of creation and the Creator has to do. It is assuredly a basic error to speak of creation myths. At best a myth may be a parallel to exact science; that is, a myth has to do with viewing what has always existed and will exist. A myth has to do with the mighty problem that at all times propounds itself to man and therefore is time- less, the problem of life and death, of sleep and wakening, of birth and dying, of morning and evening, of day and night, and so on. These are the themes of myth. Myth considers the world as it were from its frontier, but always the world which already exists. There is no creation myth because creation as such is simply not accessible to myth. Thus in the case of the Babylonian myth of creation, for example, it is quite clear that we are concerned with a myth of growth and decay which fundamentally cannot be brought into connexion with Genesis 1 and 2. At most we can say that certain mythical elements are to be found there. But what the Bible makes of that has no parallel in myth. If we are to give the biblical narrative a name, or put it in a category, then let it be that of saga. The Bible speaks in Genesis 1 and 2 of events which lie outside of our historical knowledge. But it speaks upon the basis of knowledge, which is related to history. In fact, the wonder- ful thing about the biblical creation narratives is that they stand in strict connexion with the history of Israel and so with the story of God's action in the covenant with man. According to the Old Testament narrative, this begins with God's having created heaven and earth. The first and second creation accounts alike stand plainly in connexion with the theme of the Old Testament: the first account shows the covenant in the institution of the

Sabbath as the *goal*, the second account as the *continuation* of the work of Creation.

It is impossible to separate the knowledge of God the Creator and of His work from the knowledge of God's dealings with *man*. Only when we keep before us what the triune God has done for us men in Jesus Christ can we realise what is involved in God the Creator and His work. Creation is the temporal analogue, taking place outside God, of that event in God Himself by which God is the Father of the Son. The world is not God's Son, is not 'begotten' of God; but it is *created*. But what God does as the Creator can in the Christian sense only be seen and understood as a reflection, as a shadowing forth of this inner divine relationship between God the Father and the Son. And that is why the work of creation is ascribed in the Confession to the *Father*. This does not mean that He alone is the Creator, but surely that this relationship exists between the work of creation and the relationship of Father and Son. Knowledge of creation is knowledge of God and consequently *knowledge of faith* in the deepest and ultimate sense. It is not just a vestibule in which natural theology might find a place. How should we recognise this paternity of God, were it not manifest to us in the Son? So it is not the existence of the world in its manifoldness, from which we are to read off the fact that God is its Creator. The world with its sorrow and its happiness will always be a dark mirror to us, about which we may have optimistic or pessimistic thoughts; but it gives us no information about God as the Creator. But always, when man has tried to read the truth from sun, moon and stars or from himself, the result has been an idol. But when God has been known and then known again in the world, so that the result was a joyful praise of God in creation, that is because He is to be sought and found by us in Jesus Christ. By becoming man in Jesus Christ, the fact has also become plain and credible that God is the Creator of the world. We have no alternative source of revelation.

In the article on Creator and creation the decisive point is the recognition that God does not exist for Himself, but that there is a reality distinct from Him—namely, the world. Whence do we know that? Has not each of us put to himself the question whether this entire world around us might not really be a seeming and a dream? Has not this come over you too as a fundamental doubt—not of God; that is a stupid doubt! but—of yourself? Is the whole enchantment in which we exist real? Or is not that which we regard as reality only the 'veil of Maya' and thus unreal? Is the only thing left to us just to dream this 'dream' to the end as swiftly as possible, so as to enter the Nirvana from which we derive? The statement on creation is opposed to this horrible thought. Whence can we be told authoritatively that that is a perversion and that life is not a dream but reality, that I myself am, and that the world around me is? From the standpoint of the Christian Confession there can only be one answer: this Confession tells us in its centre, in the second article, that it pleased God to become man, that in Jesus Christ we have to do with God Himself, with God the Creator, who became a creature, who existed as a creature in time and space, here, there, at that time, just as we all exist. If this is true, and this is the presupposition everything starts with, that God was in Christ, then we have a place where creation stands before us in reality and becomes recognisable. For when the Creator has Himself become a creature, God become man, if that is true (and that is the beginning of Christian knowledge), then the mystery of the Creator and His work and the mystery of His creation are open to us in Jesus Christ, and the content of the first article is plain to view. Because God has become man, the existence of creation can no longer be doubted. Gazing at Jesus Christ, with whom we live in the same space, there is told us—told as the Word of God—the Word of the Creator and the Word of His work and of the most astonishing bit of this work, of man.

The mystery of creation on the Christian interpretation is not primarily—as the fools think in their heart—the problem whether there is a God as the originator of the world; for in the Christian sense it cannot be that first of all we presuppose the reality of the world and then ask whether there is also a God. But the first thing, the thing we begin with, is God the Father and the Son and the Holy Spirit. And from that standpoint the great Christian problem is propounded, whether it can really be the case that God wishes to be not only for Himself, but that outside Him there is the world, that we exist alongside and outside Him? That is a riddle. If we make even a slight effort to look on God, to conceive Him as He reveals Himself to us, as God in mystery, God in the highest, God the Triune and Almighty, we must be astonished at the fact that there are ourselves and the world alongside and outside Him. God has no need of us, He has no need of the world and heaven and earth at all. He is rich in Himself. He has fullness of life; all glory, all beauty, all goodness and holiness reside in Him. He is sufficient unto Himself, He is God, blessed in Himself. To what end, then, the world? Here in fact there is *everything*, here in the living God. How can there be something alongside God, of which He has no need? This is the riddle of creation. And the doctrine of creation answers that God, who does not need us, created heaven and earth and myself, of 'sheer fatherly kindness and compassion, apart from any merit or worthiness of mine; for all of which I am bound to thank and praise Him, to serve Him and to be obedient, which is assuredly true'. Do you feel in these words Luther's amazement in face of creation, of the goodness of God, in which God does not will to be alone, but to have a reality beside Himself?

Creation is grace: a statement at which we should like best to pause in reverence, fear and gratitude. God does not grudge the existence of the reality distinct from Himself; He does not grudge it its own reality, nature and freedom. The existence of the creature alongside God is the great puzzle and miracle, the great question to which we must and may give an answer, the answer given us through God's Word; it is the genuine question about existence, which is essentially and fundamentally distinguished from the question which rests upon error, 'Is there a God?' That there is a world is the most unheard-of thing, the miracle of the grace of God. Is it not true that if we confront existence, not least our own existence, we can but in astonishment state the truth and reality of the fact that I *may exist*, the world may exist, although it is a reality distinct from God, although the world including man and therefore myself is not God? God in the highest, the Triune God, the Father, the Almighty, is not arbitrary; He does not grudge existence to this other. He not only does not grudge it him, He not only leaves it to him, He gives it him. We exist and heaven and earth exist in their complete, supposed infinity, because God gives them existence. That is the great statement of the first article.

But this means also that since God does not grudge this world its existence, its own reality, nature and freedom, this implies that this world is not God Himself, as pantheistic confusion again and again wishes to assert. It is not that we are God; but it can never be anything but our disastrous error that 'we should like to be as God'. It is therefore not, as ancient and modern gnosis claims, that what the Bible calls the Son is fundamentally the created world, or that the world is by nature God's child. Nor is it that the world is to be understood as an outflow, an emanation from God, as something divine which wells out of God like a stream out of a spring. That would really not be creation, but a living movement of God, an expression of Himself. But creation means something different; it means a reality distinct from God. And, finally, the world must not be understood as a manifestation of God, so that God would be to some extent the Idea. God who alone is real and essential and free, is one; and heaven and earth, man and the universe are something else, and this something else is not God, though it exists through God. So this other thing is not based independently on itself, as though the world had its own principle, and thus was on its own feet and independent, so that from its standpoint there might be a God, but a God far away and separated from it, so that there would be two realms and two worlds: on the one side this world with its own reality and lawfulness, and quite elsewhere and otherwise God as well, His kingdom and His world, perhaps to be depicted in very fine rich hues, perhaps also in a relation between here and beyond, perhaps in such a way as for it to be granted to man to be on the way from here to there. But this world would not be by God's agency, would not be from Him and thus would not completely belong to Him and be grounded in Him.

No; what God does not grudge the world is creaturely reality, a creaturely nature and creaturely freedom, an existence appropriate to the creation, the world. The world is no appearance, it exists, but it exists by way of creation. It can, it may exist alongside of God, by God's agency. Creaturely reality means reality on the basis of a *creatio ex nihilo*, a creation out of nothing. Where nothing exists—and not a kind of primal matter—there through God there has come into existence that which is distinct from Him. And since there is now something, since we exist because of divine grace, we must never forget that, as the basis of our existence and of the existence of the whole world, there is in the background that divine—not just *facere*, but—*creation*. Everything outside God is held constant by God over nothingness. Creaturely nature means existence in time and space, existence with a beginning and an end, existence that becomes, in order to pass away again. Once it was not, and once it will no longer be. And it is not one but many. As there is a once and a now, there is also a here and a there. The world, in this process, is called time, and, in this separateness, space. But God is eternal. That does not mean that there is no time in Him, but it is a different time from ours; for fundamentally we never have presence, and for us spatiality means apartness. God's time and space are free from the limitations in which alone time and space are thinkable for us. God is the Lord of time and the Lord of space. As He is the origin of these forms too, nothing in Him has any limitation or imperfection, such as pertains to creaturely existence.

And creaturely freedom means, finally, that there is a contingency of what is, a specific existence of the creature; and this specific existence, at any rate of the human creature, means freedom to decide, ability to act one way or another. But this freedom can only be the freedom appropriate to the creature, which possesses its reality not of itself, and which has its nature in time and space. Since it is real freedom, it is established and limited by the subjection to law, which prevails in the universe and is again and again discernible; it is limited by the existence of its fellow creatures, and on the other hand by the sovereignty of God. For if we are free, it is only because our Creator is the infinitely free. All human freedom is but an imperfect mirroring of the divine freedom.

The creature is threatened by the possibility of nothingness and of destruction, which is excluded by God—and only by God. If a creature exists, it is only maintained in its mode of existence if God so wills. If He did not so will, nothingness would inevitably break in from all sides. The creature itself could not rescue and preserve itself. And man's freedom to decide, as it is given to man by God, is not a freedom to decide between good and evil. Man is not made to be Hercules at the cross-roads. Evil does not lie in the possibilities of the God-created creature. Freedom to decide means freedom to decide towards the Only One for whom God's creature can decide, for the affirmation of Him who has created it, for the accomplishment of His will; that is, for obedience. But we have to do with *freedom* to decide. And here too danger threatens. Should it happen that the creature makes a different use of his freedom than the only possible one, should he want to sin—that is, to 'sunder' himself from God and from himself—what else can happen than that, entered into contradiction to God's will, he is *bound* to fall by his disobedience, by the impossibility of this disobedience, into this possibility not foreseen in creation? Now to be in time and space must cause his destruction; now for him this coming and passing away, this here and there in his existence must mean the reverse of salvation. There must now take place the fall into *nihil*. Could it be otherwise? I am speaking here now of this, in order to make clear that this whole realm that we term evil—death, sin, the Devil and hell—is *not* God's creation, but rather what was excluded by God's creation, that to which God has said 'No'. And if there is a reality of evil, it can only be the reality of this excluded and repudiated thing, the reality behind God's back, which He passed over, when He made the world and made it good. 'And God saw everything that He had made, and behold it was very good.' What is not good God did not make; it has no creaturely existence. But if being is to be ascribed to it at all, and we would rather not say that it is non-existent, then it is only the power of the being which arises out of the weight of the divine 'No'. We must not look for darkness in God Himself. He is the Father of light. If we begin to speak of a *Deus absconditus*, we are speaking of an idol. God the Creator is He who does not grudge the creature its existence. And what is in being, what is in truth real, is by this favour of God.

God's Word is the power of all creaturely being. God creates, rules and sustains it as the theatre of His glory. I should like by this to point to the *ground* and the *goal* of creation, which are in the end one and the same thing.

The *ground* of creation is God's grace, and the fact that there is a grace of God is real and present to us, alive and powerful in God's Word. By God speaking and having spoken His Word in the history of Israel, in Jesus Christ, in the foundation of the Church of Jesus Christ and right up to this day, and by His speaking to all futurity, the creation was and is and will be. What exists *exists*, because it exists not of itself, but by God's Word, for His Word's sake, in the sense and in the purpose of His Word. God upholds all things (*ta panta*) by His Word (Heb. 1. 2; cf. John 1. 1 f. and Col. 1). The whole was made by Him for its own sake. The Word which is attested for us in Holy Scripture, the story of Israel, of Jesus Christ and His Church, is the first thing, and the whole world with its light and shadow, its depths and its heights is the second. By the Word the world exists. A marvellous reversal of our whole thinking! Don't let yourselves be led astray by the difficulty of the time-concept, which might well result from this. The world came into being, it was created and sustained by the little child that was born in Bethlehem, by the Man who died on the Cross of Golgotha, and the third day rose again. *That* is the Word of creation, by which all things were brought into being. That is where the *meaning* of creation comes from, and that is why it says at the beginning of the Bible: 'In the beginning God made heaven and earth and God said, 'Let there be . . .'. This unheard-of utterance of God in that uncanny first chapter of the Bible! Think of this utterance, not as a magic word of an Almighty, who now let the world go forth, but listen: God speaks concretely, as Scripture attests; and since this was God's reality from the beginning, everything that is came into being— the light and heaven and earth, plants and beasts, and last of all, man.

And if we inquire into the *goal* of creation, the object of the whole, the object of heaven and earth and all creation, I can only say that it is to be the theatre of His glory. The meaning is that God is being glorified. *Doxa*, *gloria*, means quite simply to become manifest. God wills to be visible in the world; and to that extent creation is a significant action of God. 'Behold, it was very good.' Whatever objections may be raised against the reality of the world, its goodness incontestably consists in the fact that it may be the theatre of His glory, and man the witness to this glory. We must not desire to know *a priori* what goodness is, or to grumble if the world does not correspond to it. For the purpose for which God made the world it is also good. 'The theatre of His glory, *theatrum gloriae Dei*', says Calvin of it. But man is the witness; he who is allowed to be where God is made glorious, is not a merely passive witness; the witness has to express what he has seen. That is man's nature, that is what he is able to do, to be a witness of God's acts. This purpose of God 'justifies' Him as the Creator.

9

HEAVEN AND EARTH

Heaven is the creation inconceivable to man, earth the creation conceivable to him. He himself is the creature on the boundary between heaven and earth. The covenant between God and man is the meaning and the glory, the ground and the goal of heaven and earth and the whole creation.

'CREATOR of Heaven and Earth', says the Confession. We may and indeed we must say, that in the two concepts of heaven and earth, single and in their conjunction, we are confronted with what we might term the Christian doctrine of the creature. But these two concepts do not signify a kind of equivalent to what we usually call to-day a picture of the world, even though it can be said that somewhat of the old picture of the world is reflected in them. But it is not the business of Holy Scripture or of Christian faith, with which we have to occupy ourselves here, to represent a definite world-picture. The Christian faith is bound neither to an old nor to a modern world-picture. The Christian Confession has in course of the centuries passed through more than one world-picture. And its representatives were always ill-advised when they believed that this or that world-picture was an adequate expression for what the Church, apart from creation, has to think. Christian faith is fundamentally free in regard to all world-pictures, that is, to all attempts to regard what exists by the measure and with the means of the dominant science of the time. As Christians we must not let ourselves be taken captive either by an ancient picture of this nature or one newly arisen and beginning to be dominant. And above all we must not combine the Church's business with this or that *Weltanschauung*. *Weltanschauung* means something still more comprehensive than world-picture, since in it a so-called philosophico-metaphysical conception of man is added to the harmony. We must beware as Christians, and the Church must beware of establishing itself on the basis of any sort of *Weltanschauung*. For *Weltanschauung* is very near 'religion'. But by the decisive content of the Bible, Jesus Christ, we are by no means enjoined to adopt a

59

Weltanschauung for our own. We Christians are once for all dispensed from attempting, by starting from ourselves, to understand what exists, or to reach the cause of things and with or without God to reach a general view. So my advice would be, that if you are faced with any such general view, you should bracket it, even if it should be called a *Christian Weltanschauung*. Perhaps this warning should be expressed with special emphasis in the *German* sphere! (The word *Weltanschauung*, like the word *Blitzkrieg*, exists only in the German tongue. Englishmen must, significantly, quote it in German, if they wish to use it.)

It is quite remarkable that the content of creation is described here by heaven and earth. 'In the beginning God made heaven and earth'; from this first statement of the Bible the Confession has taken these two concepts. Nevertheless, we may ask ourselves whether and to what extent these two concepts are adequate to describe creation. In his small catechism, Luther made the attempt to pass beyond them, by writing, in the explanation of the first article, that 'I believe that God has created *me*, together with all creatures. . . .' So in place of heaven and earth Luther has put man, and that in the quite concrete pointedness of 'me'. This alteration or slight correction of the Creed assuredly has its own good sense. Straightway we are pointed to the creature with whom the Creed is essentially concerned—to man. But why does the Creed say it differently? Why does it speak of heaven and earth and not of man at all? Are we to stick to Luther, or do we prefer to say that there is something majestic in the way in which in the Creed man is completely passed over, in which he appears as quite unimportant? Or should we try—and I would say 'Yes'— to consider the matter in this way, that our subject being heaven and earth, the place is unsurpassably depicted to which man belongs? By the very fact that in the first instance he is not the thing we are speaking of, is not man spoken of indirectly in a very impressive manner? Heaven and earth describe an arena prepared for a quite definite event, in the centre of which, from our standpoint of course, stands man. Is not this precisely a description of the creation, which in its content thus points decisively towards him? What is certain is that by this description we realise that heaven and earth are not a reality in themselves, which are understandable and explicable in terms of themselves, but that they, with man in the centre, as the meaning of their existence, derive *from God*, belong to God, and that in the sense of the Christian Creed as summarising creation they are meant to be regarded in their connexion with God, His will and His action. Here is the fundamental difference between all *Weltanschauungen* and what Holy Scripture and faith have to say. In a *Weltanschauung* we start from what is, as being the meaning, in order to step up from the depths to the conception of a God; but in Holy Scripture we have to do with heaven and earth and with man solely in the context of 'I believe in God the Creator of Heaven and earth'. In this genitive it is made manifest that I believe not in creation, but in God, the Creator.

Heaven is the creation inconceivable to man; earth is the creation conceivable to him. I concur, therefore, in the explanation of heaven and earth, given in the Nicene Creed, as *visibilia et invisibilia*.

I mean to reproduce this 'visible' and 'invisible' by 'conceivable' and 'inconceivable'. When Holy Scripture, with whose usage we here link up, speaks of heaven, we are not to understand by that simply what we usually term heaven, the atmospheric or even stratospheric heaven, but a creaturely reality, which is utterly superior to this 'heaven'. In the world-picture of antiquity, particularly in that of the Near East, the visible world was thought to be spanned by a huge bell-shaped bowl, the so-called firmament. This firmament from our standpoint constitutes, so to speak, the beginning of heaven, a reality we cannot see. Above the firmament there comes a tremendous ocean, which is separated from the earth by the firmament. It is only above this ocean that the third, the real heaven comes, which constitutes the throne of God. I mention this only in order to show you what idea, in the sense of a picture of the world, stands behind the biblical concept of heaven: a reality which confronts man, but is also utterly superior to him, yet as a creaturely reality. This entire 'beyond' which is withdrawn from man and confronts him, in part menacingly, in part gloriously, must not of course be confused with God. When we have reached what to us is inconceivable, we have not yet reached God, but merely heaven. If we wanted to call this inconceivable reality God, we should be playing at deification of the creature no less than when a so-called 'primitive man' worships the sun. Very many philosophers have been guilty of such deification of the creature. The boundary of our conceiving is not the boundary that separates us from God, but solely the boundary which the Creed calls the boundary between heaven and earth. There exists within creation this reality which to us is simply a mystery, the heavenly reality. It has nothing to do with God, but a lot to do with the creation made by God. Within creation as well we are faced by an inconceivable mystery, by depths of being which may alternately terrify and delight us. The philosophers and poets who have spoken and sung of this mystery were not wrong. Even as Christians we may recognise this—existence has its depths and it has its heights—here and now we are surrounded by mysteries of every kind, and well for the man who knows that there are more things in heaven and earth, than are dreamt of in your philosophy! Creation itself has a heavenly component overhead; but it is not to be feared and worshipped as a thing divine. In a world which has these heavenly components we are symbolically reminded by them of the Reality which is above us in quite a different way than heaven, of the supra-heavenly Reality, of the Creator of earth and heaven. But let us not confuse the sign with the thing itself.

Over against this upper creation stands the lower creation, the earth, as the content of the creation conceivable by us, as creation inside the boundary, within which we are able in the broadest sense to see and to hear and to feel, to think and to contemplate. Everything contained within the realm of our human and of our spiritual capacity, as well as all that we can conceive intuitively, is, in the sense of the Christian Creed, the earth. To the earth, then, belongs also what the philosopher calls the world of reason or ideas. There are also in this lower world differentiations between the physical and the spiritual, which are, however, differentiations within the earthly world. It is within this earthly world that man has his origin; God took man from the earth. The world of man, the space for his existence and his history, and at the same time man's natural goal as well, 'to earth thou shalt return': that is the earth. If man does have another origin than this earthly one, and another goal than that of returning to the earth again, then it is on the basis of the reality of the covenant between God and man. We start talking of the grace of God when we ascribe more to man than earthly existence, in which is included that the earth is under heaven. There is no world of man *in abstracto*. It would be an error if man were not clear that his conceivable world is bounded by an inconceivable one. Well for us that there are children and poets and philosophers, who are continually reminding us of this higher side of historical reality. The earthly world is really only one side of creation. But in the heavenly as little as in the earthly realm are we already in the realm of God; and so the first and second commandments hold good: 'Thou shalt not make unto thee any image nor any sort of likeness, either of what is in heaven or of what is on earth. . . .' Neither on earth nor in heaven is there any divine power which we have to love or to fear.

Man is the creature of the boundary between heaven and earth; he is on earth and under heaven. He is the being that conceives his environment, who can see, hear, understand and dominate it: 'Thou hast put all things under his feet.' He is the essence of a free being in this earthly world. And the same creature stands beneath heaven; and in face of the *invisibilia*, of what he cannot conceive or dispose of, he does not dominate but is completely dependent. Man knows about his earthly fellow-creature, because he is so unknowing in face of the heavenly world. At this inner boundary of creation stands man, as though even as a creature he had to represent this above and below, and thus, as a creature, to signify his place in a relationship which penetrates into the heights and the depths in quite a different way from that of heaven and earth. Man is the place within creation where the creature in its fullness is concentrated, and at the same time stretches beyond itself; the place where God wishes to be praised within creation, and may be praised.

But we would not have said the last decisive word about creation, if we did not add that the covenant between God and man is the meaning and the glory, the ground and the goal of heaven and earth and so of the whole creation. With this we seem, but only seem, to reach out beyond the realm of knowledge and of the first article of the Confession. For by covenant we mean Jesus Christ. But it is not the case that the covenant between God and man is so to speak a second fact, something additional, but the covenant is as old as creation itself. When the existence of creation begins, God's dealing with man also begins. For all that exists points towards man, in so far as it makes God's purpose visible, moving towards His revealed and effective action in the covenant with Jesus Christ. The covenant is not only quite as old as creation; it is older than it. Before the world was, before heaven and earth were, the resolve or decree of God exists in view of this event in which God willed to hold communion with man, as it became inconceivably true and real in Jesus Christ. And when we ask about the meaning of existence and creation, about their ground and goal, we have to think of this covenant between God and man.

And now if we glance back at this lapidary description of creation, of heaven and earth, and man the boundary between the two, then without being over bold and without being guilty of speculation, we may now say that heaven and earth are related like God and man in the covenant, so that even the existence of creation as such is a single, mighty *signum*, a sign of the will of God. The meeting and the togetherness of above and below, of the conceivable and the inconceivable, of the infinite and the limited —we are speaking of creation. All that is the world. But since within this world there really exist an above and a below confronting one another, since in every breath we take, in every one of our thoughts, in every great and petty experience of our human lives heaven and earth are side by side, greeting each other, attracting and repelling each other and yet belonging to one another, we are, in our existence, of which God is the Creator, a sign and indication, a promise of what ought to happen in creation and to creation—the meeting, the togetherness, the fellowship and, in Jesus Christ, the oneness of Creator and creature.

10

JESUS CHRIST

*The heart of the object of Christian faith is the word of the act in
which God from all eternity willed to become man in Jesus Christ
for our good, did become man in time for our good, and will be and
remain man in eternity for our good. This work of the Son of God
includes in itself the work of the Father as its presupposition and the
work of the Holy Spirit as its consequence.*

WITH this paragraph we pass into the heart of the Christian
confession, whose text is indeed distinguished by particular
explicitness and which is not only outwardly the heart of it all.
Even in our introduction to these lectures, when we were speaking
of faith, and in the first lecture, when we spoke of God the Father,
the Almighty, Creator of heaven and earth, we could not avoid
continually pointing to this centre. We could not possibly have
given a genuine exposition of the first article without continually
interpreting it by means of the second. Indeed, the second
article does not just follow the first, nor does it just precede
the third; but it is the fountain of light by which the other
two are lit. It is also susceptible of historical proof, that the
Christian Confession arose out of a shorter and indeed probably
a quite short primitive form, which included only what we
confess to-day in the second article. It is believed that the original
Christian confession consisted of the three words, 'Jesus Christ
(is) Lord', to which were only later added the first and third
articles. This historical event was not arbitrary. It is also materi-
ally significant to know that historically the second article is the
source of the whole. A Christian is one who makes confession of
Christ. And Christian confession is confession of Jesus Christ the
Lord.

Starting with this heart of the Christian Confession, all that it
expresses of God the Father and God the Holy Spirit is to be
regarded as an expanding statement. When Christian theologians
wished to sketch a theology of God the Creator abstractly and
directly, they have always gone astray, even when in tremendous
reverence they tried to think and speak of this high God. And

the same thing took place, when the theologians tried to push
through to a theology of the third article, to a theology of the
Spirit, to a theology of experience as opposed to the theology of
the high God in the first article. Then too they have gone astray.
Perhaps the whole of modern theology, as characteristically found
in Schleiermacher, could be, must be understood as theology prepared by certain developments in the seventeenth and eighteenth
centuries. It became a one-sided theology of the third article,
which believed that it might venture with the Holy Spirit alone,
without reflecting that the third article is only the explication
of the second, the declaration of what Jesus Christ our Lord
means for us men. Starting with Jesus Christ and with Him alone,
we must see and understand what in the Christian sense is involved
by the mighty relationship, to which we can only point again and
again in sheer amazement, about which we cannot help being
in danger of great error, when we say, *God and man*. What
we mean by that can only be declared adequately, by our
confessing that 'Jesus is Christ'. And as for what is involved in
the relationship between creation and the reality of existence on
the one hand, and on the other hand the Church, redemption,
God—that can never be understood from any general truth
about our existence, nor from the reality of history of religion;
this we can only learn from the relation between Jesus and
Christ. Here we see clearly what is meant by 'God *above* man'
(Article I) and 'God *with* man' (Article III). That is why Article
II, why Christology, is the touchstone of all knowledge of
God in the Christian sense, the touchstone of all theology. 'Tell
me how it stands with your Christology, and I shall tell you
who you are.' This is the point at which ways diverge, and the
point at which is fixed the relation between theology and philosophy, and the relation between knowledge of God and knowledge of men, the relation between revelation and reason, the
relation between Gospel and Law, the relation between God's
truth and man's truth, the relation between outer and inner, the
relation between theology and politics. At this point everything
becomes clear or unclear, bright or dark. For here we are standing at the centre. And however high and mysterious and difficult
everything we want to know might seem to us, yet we may also
say that this is just where everything becomes quite simple, quite
straightforward, quite childlike. Right here in this centre, in
which as a Professor of Systematic Theology I must call to you,

'Look! This is the point now! Either knowledge, or the greatest folly!'—here I am in front of you, like a teacher in Sunday school facing his kiddies, who has something to say which a mere four-year-old can really understand. 'The world was lost, but Christ was born, rejoice, O Christendom!'

This centre is the Word of the act or the act of the Word. I greatly desire to make it clear to you, that in this centre of Christian faith the whole contrast, so current among us, between word and work, between knowing and living, ceases to have any meaning. But the Word, the Logos, is actually the work, the *ergon*, as well; the *verbum* is also the *opus*. Where God and this centre of our faith are involved, those differences which seem so interesting and important to us, become not just superfluous but silly. It is the truth of the real or the reality of the true which here enters the field: God speaks, God acts, God is in the midst. The very Word with which we are here concerned is an act, this act, which as such is the Word, is Revelation.

When we pronounce the name of Jesus Christ, we are not speaking of an idea. The name Jesus Christ is not the transparent shell, through which we glimpse something higher—no room for Platonism here! What is involved is this actual name and this title; this person is involved. Not any chance person, not a 'chance reality in history' in Lessing's sense. The 'chance fact of history' is just the eternal truth of reason! Nor does this name Jesus Christ indicate a result of human history. It was invariably a human discovery, when the effort was made to show that the whole of human history was bound to have its culminating point in Jesus Christ. Not for one moment was it possible to say that of the history of Israel, not to mention world-history. Of course in retrospect we may and must say that here history is fulfilled. But fulfilled in a truth which, looked at from the standpoint of all historical results, is completely novel and offensive! To the Greeks foolishness, to the Jews a stumbling-block. So in the name of Jesus Christ we have not to do with the result of a postulate of man, with the product of a human need, with the figure of a redeemer and saviour to be explained and derived from man's guilt. Even the fact that he is a sinner cannot be known from man himself. It is rather the result of knowing Jesus Christ; in His light we see the light and in this light our own darkness. Everything that deserves to be called knowledge in the Christian sense lives from the knowledge of Jesus Christ.

Also from the standpoint of the first article it is something quite new when we say, 'I believe in Jesus Christ'. God, the Creator of heaven and earth, the eternal God in His loftiness and hidden-ness, in His inconceivability, which transcends the inconceivability of the heavenly reality, is confessed in the first article. And now here in the second article the apparently contradictory, at all events the quite new thing is confessed, which for the first time makes clear and illustrates the loftiness and inconceivability of God in the first article, and at the same time confronts us with a tremendous riddle, that God has form. A name sounds forth, a man stands before us in God's place. Here the Almighty appears not almighty at all. We were told of God's eternity and omnipresence. Now we are told of a here and now, of a happening on a small scale in the midst of human history, of a story at the beginning of our era, at a definite place on our earth. In the first article we were told about God the Father; and now from the unity of the Godhead God Himself comes forth in the form of the *Son*. Now God is this Other in God and proceeding from God. The Creator who is distinguished from all that is, and the creature as the essence of all being which is different from the being of God, are described in the first article. And now the second article says that the Creator Himself became a creature. He, the eternal God, became—not creation in its totality, but—*one* creature.

'He who from eternity willed to become man for our good, has become man in time for our good, will be and remain man in eternity for our good'—that is, Jesus Christ. The English novelist, Dorothy L. Sayers, who has recently turned to theology with remarkable interest, has described in a pamphlet how unheard-of, how strange, how 'interesting' the narrative is of the fact that God became man. Imagine for a moment this story being one day put in the papers! It really is a sensational story, more sensational than anything else. And that is the centre of Christianity, this infinitely surprising thing, that never existed before and cannot be repeated.

At all times there have been combinations of these two concepts, God and man. The idea of incarnation is not alien to mythology. But the thing that distinguishes the Christian message from this idea is that all myths are basically just the exposition of an idea, of a general truth. A myth circles round the relation between day and night, winter and spring, death and life; it always implies a timeless reality. The message of Jesus Christ has nothing to do with this myth; it is formally distinguished from it by its possessing the unique historical conception that it is said of an historical human being that it happened in His existence that God was made man, that consequently His existence was identical with the existence of God. The Christian message is a historical message. And only by seeing eternity and time together, God and man, only then do we grasp what is expressed by the name Jesus Christ. Jesus Christ is the reality of the covenant between God and man. It is only when we look at Jesus Christ that we succeed, in the sense of the first article, in speaking about God in the highest; because it is here that we get to know man in the covenant with this God, in His concrete form as this man. And when in the third article of the Confession we may speak and hear of God in man, of God who acts with us and in us, it might be in itself an ideology, a description of human enthusiasm, an over-wrought idea of the meaning of man's inner life with its transports and its experiences, a projection of what takes place in us men into the height of an imaginary deity, which we call Holy Spirit. But if we look at the covenant which God has really concluded with us men, then we know that it is not so. God on high is really near to us men in the depths. God is present. We may make bold to speak of a reality of the Holy Spirit in view of this covenant between God and man, in which God became man, in this one who stands for all others.

'God became man for thy good, O man. 'Tis God's own Child that binds Himself to thine own blood.' This Christmas truth I have tried to describe in its three elements. We must start with the historical reality, that time, our time, has an historical centre, from which it is to be understood, from which, for all its contradictions, for all its heights and depths, it stands in a relationship to God. In the midst of time it happened that God became man for our good. While underlining the uniqueness of this event, we have to reflect that this was not an accident, not one historical event among others. But it is the event which God willed from eternity. Here the second article reaches back to the realm of the first; here creation and redemption are united. From this standpoint we must say that creation itself, God's existence itself, prior to the whole world from eternity, is unthinkable apart from His will as it has been fulfilled and revealed in time. The eternal will of God has this form. From eternity there is no other God than the God whose will was revealed in this act and in this Word. Do not regard that as a speculation. The Christ message is, let me repeat, not one truth among others; it is *the* truth. In thinking of God, we have from the beginning to think of the name of Jesus Christ. 'And who in eternity for our good will be and remain man'—the truth of the covenant, the unity of God and man, by being an historical truth which became real at that time and place, is no transitory truth. Jesus Christ is the king whose kingdom hath no end. 'Just as thou wert before all time, abidest Thou in eternity.' So we confront God. God really encompasses us in Jesus Christ 'on every side'. Here there is no escape. But there is also no drop into nothingness. In pronouncing the name of Jesus Christ we are on a way. 'I am the way, the truth and the life.' That is the way through time, the centre of which He is; and this way has an origin which lies not in darkness. This way does not proceed out of darkness; its origin corresponds with this way. And it leads to a goal, which once more is not dark; the very future bears His name, Jesus Christ. It is He who was and is and is to come, as it says at the end of the second article, 'from whence He shall come to judge the quick and the dead'. He is the Alpha and the Omega, the beginning and the end. So also the middle, so also the way. We are upheld on all sides and indeed uplifted, when we pronounce this name, Jesus Christ, in the sense of the Confession.

And all this 'for our good'. This may not be suppressed. In this covenant, this revelation, we are really not concerned with a miracle and a mystery, perhaps interesting and remarkable, confronting our existence—that of course is also involved; but we should not have understood the matter, if we wanted to make it the object of a mere intellectual spectacle. Mere gnosis would be —even if we would adduce the whole New Testament in proof and speak of Christ with ever so lofty words—a sounding brass and a tinkling cymbal. Melanchthon was right when he said (*Loci* of 1521), what in later theology was so frequently misquoted: *Hoc est Christum cognoscere—beneficia Christi cognoscere.* The misuse of this, particularly in the school of Ritschl, consisted in a refusal to recognise the high mystery of the Incarnation, and the desire instead to speak of Christ merely as a Being from whom certain benefits accrue to man, which have a definite 'value' for him. We cannot speak *in abstracto* of the *beneficia Christi*. We must know His *beneficia* in action in order to know Him.

The benefit consists altogether in this reality of revelation, that God was made man for the good of me, a man. In that way we are helped. The kingdom of heaven does exist already; from God's side action has been already taken for our good. To pronounce the name of Jesus Christ means to acknowledge that we are cared for, that we are not lost. Jesus Christ is man's salvation in all circumstances and in face of all that darkens his life, including the evil that proceeds from himself. There is nothing which is not already made good in this happening, that God became man for our good. Anything that is left can be no more than the discovery of this fact. We do not exist in any kind of gloomy uncertainty; we exist through the God who was gracious to us before we existed at all. It may be true that we exist in contradiction to this God, that we live in remoteness from Him, indeed in hostility to Him. It is still truer that God has prepared reconciliation for us, before we entered the struggle against Him. And true though it may be that in connexion with our alienation from God man can only be regarded as a lost being, it is still much truer that God has so acted for our good, does and will so act, that there exists salvation for every lost condition. It is this faith that we are called to believe through the Christian Church and in the Holy Spirit. Indeed the fact is that everything that we have to bewail and everything that can be brought against us as a necessary and justifiable complaint, that all sighing and all misery and all despair—and there truly is cause for it all—is distinguished from all more or less chance trouble by the fact that complaint and accusation, which again and again break out from the depths of creation, actually acquire strength from our recognition that we men are the object of the divine compassion. Only from the depths of all that God has done for us can it be made clear that we find ourselves in misery. Who then is aware of man's real wretchedness, save he who is aware of God's mercy?

This work of the Son of God includes the work of the Father as its presupposition and the work of the Holy Spirit as its consequence. The first article is to a certain extent the source, the third article the goal of our path. But the second article is the Way upon which we find ourselves in faith. From that vantage we may review the entire fullness of the acts of God.

II

THE SAVIOUR AND SERVANT OF GOD

The name Jesus and the title Christ express the election, the Person and the work of the Man in whom the prophetic, priestly and kingly mission of the nation Israel is revealed and set forth.

IN the two foreign words with which the second article begins and with which its entire content is connected, Jesus Christ, we are concerned with a personal name and with a title, with the name of a definite man and with the description of His office. And in pronouncing this name and this title, 'Jesus the Christ', we find ourselves in the first instance in the area of the history and language of the nation Israel. The special theme which must occupy us to-day is Jesus, this man of Israel, the man who reveals and sets forth, in a definite function, the nature and mission of Israel. Now, the position is very peculiar, since the personal name, Jesus, belongs to the realm of the Hebrew language; Jesus is an equivalent of the name which frequently turns up in the Old Testament and once, indeed, in a very emphatic way, as Joshua. But the title Christ is Greek, although the Greek translation of a Hebrew word Messiah, the Anointed. So in these two words to a certain extent a history is indicated. A Jew, an Israelite, a Hebrew, Jesus who is the Christ—that is a bit of earthly history, which takes place on the way from Israel to the Greeks, that is, to the whole world. We cannot split Jesus Christ and seek to retain only one of the two components. Jesus Christ would not be what He is, were He not the Christ, the Commissioner who comes out of *Israel*, who is the *Jew* Jesus. But again this Jew Jesus would not be the person He is, were He not God's Commissioner, were He not Christ who causes Israel's life and meaning to gleam as a light in the Gentile world and in the whole of humanity. If we would see and understand Jesus Christ, we must be continually striving to understand the two things, this starting-point and this goal. Wherever the one or the other is forgotten or actually denied, we no longer have dealings with Him.

The personal name Jesus really means in English 'Jehovah (the God of Israel) helps'. The official title of Christ or Messiah described in the Judaism of the time of Jesus a man expected by Israel, due to come in the last days, who was to reveal God's glory, God's hitherto hidden although promised glory. It described the man who was to free Israel, which for centuries was sunk in need and oppression, and, himself a man of Israel, to rule over the nations. When Jesus of Nazareth arose and preached and took His way out of the narrowness of Nazareth in the first instance into the spaciousness of the history of His own nation, which as in olden times was to find its fulfilment in Jerusalem, then the mystery of this figure, of this son of Joseph of Nazareth, was that He was the Messiah, this expected One in the last days, that He revealed Himself as such and was recognised as such. The name Jesus ('God helps', the Saviour) was a familiar name, and there were many of this name; and One of these many, because God so willed and disposed, was the unique person in whom the divine promise proceeded to fulfilment. And at the same time this fulfilment signifies the fulfilment of what was given to Israel, and the fulfilment and revelation of what this people was appointed to be for the history of the whole world, of all nations, in fact of the whole of humanity. He was not named Jesus Messiah by the first community, but Jesus Christ. Therein is revealed, therein is opened the door into the world. But there remains the Jewish name *Jesus*. His way into the spaciousness of the world leads out from the narrowness of Israel.

Perhaps you are surprised at my laying such stress on the name and title. We must be quite clear that in the whole of antiquity and also in Israel names and titles were not quite so external and incidental, as they, are for us. This name and this title express something; and this must be understood in a quite concrete way: they are *revelation*. So they are not a mere designating or naming, an ornament which the person named might or might not wear. It was the angel who said to Mary, 'Thou shalt call thy Son Jesus, God helps, Saviour, *Soter!*' Nor is the title Christ to be regarded as the expression of some human deliberation, but it necessarily belongs to this man. This title is not to be separated from the Bearer of this name; the Bearer of this name is born in order to carry this title. There is no dualism between name and calling. At His very birth this title was so to speak lowered on to Him inevitably, like a crown, so that this person does not exist apart from this office, nor this office apart from this person. He is *the* Joshua, the 'God helps', because He is chosen for the work and office of the Christ, the prophetic, priestly and kingly Servant of God out of Israel.

We must pause a moment in face of the fact—for it is certainly important—that in this Jesus Christ we are dealing with the man in whom the mission of this one people, the people of Israel, the Jewish people, is set forth and revealed. Christ, the Servant of God who came from it, and the figure of God's Servant for all peoples, as well as this one people of Israel, are two realities inseparable from each other, not only at that time but for the whole of history, indeed for all eternity. Israel is nothing apart from Jesus Christ; but we also have to say that Jesus Christ would not be Jesus Christ apart from Israel. So first of all we must look for a moment at this Israel, in order to be able really to look at Jesus Christ.

The people Israel, the people of the Old Testament, are the people with whom God has concluded a *covenant*, which is repeated in ever new forms in the course of their history. It is here in Israel that this concept of the covenant between God and man has its source and seat. Just because the covenant of God with man is once and for all His covenant with the people Israel, it is distinct from a philosophical idea, from a universally human idea. Here we are concerned not with any idea or notion, but with the fact that God called Abraham out of the nations, and bound Himself to him and to his family, his 'seed'. The whole history of the Old Testament and so of the people Israel is nothing but the story of this covenant between God and this people, between this people and God who bears the name of Jehovah. When we recognise that the Christian faith and the Christian message is directed to all men, that it proclaims the God who is the God of the whole world, we must also see that the way to the general, universal truth that embraces the whole world and all men, is the way of particularity, in which God, in a way which seems strange and arbitrary, is the God of Abraham, Isaac and Jacob. This nation of Israel, as the Old Testament presents it to us, in its election and calling, in its unique distinctiveness, though also in its folly, in its perversity and weakness, as the object of the ever new love and goodness of God, but also as the object of the judgments of God that affected this people in unheard-of ways—this nation embodies in history the free grace of God for us all. We are not concerned here just with an historic fact; but in this relation of the free grace of God with Israel, with the Jewish people, we are concerned, not with a matter which we Christians deriving from the heathen, we Greeks, Germans and Gauls might point back to, as something that has ceased to affect us, so that the Christendom of to-day might turn out to be, as it were, a balloon trip, separated from the history of Israel. If as Christians we thought that Church and Synagogue no longer affected one another, everything would be lost. And where this separation between the community and the Jewish nation has been made complete, it is the Christian community which has suffered. The whole reality of the revelation of God is then secretly denied and as an inevitable result philosophy and ideology take the upper hand, and Christianity of a Greek or a German or some other freely chosen kind in invented. (I am quite aware that there has at all times also existed something like a Swiss Christianity, which certainly was and is no better than the German one!)

Do you know the story in which the significance of the Jewish nation is best summarised? Frederick the Great once asked his personal physician Zimmermann of Brugg in Aargau: 'Zimmermann, can you name me a single proof of the existence of God?' And Zimmermann replied, 'Your Majesty, the Jews!' By that he meant that if one wanted to ask for a proof of God, for something visible and tangible, that no one could contest, which is unfolded before the eyes of all men, then we should have to turn to the Jews. Quite simply, there they are to the present day. Hundreds of little nations in the Near East have disappeared, all other Semitic tribes of that time have dissolved and disappeared in the huge sea of nations; and this one tiny nation has maintained itself. And when to-day we speak of Semitism or anti-Semitism, we think of the tiny nation, which remarkably still keeps to the fore, is still recognisable, physically and spiritually, so that again and again we can say that this man is a non-Aryan or else that he is a half or a quarter non-Aryan. In fact, if the question of a proof of God is raised, one need merely point to this simple historical fact. For in the person of the Jew there stands a witness before our eyes, the witness of God's covenant with Abraham, Isaac and Jacob and in that way with us all. Even one who does not understand Holy Scripture can see this reminder.

And don't you see, the remarkable theological importance, the extraordinary spiritual and sacred significance of the National Socialism that now lies behind us is that right from its roots it was anti-Semitic, that in this movement it was realised with a simply demonic clarity, that *the* enemy is the *Jew*. Yes, the enemy in this matter had to be a Jew. In this Jewish nation there really lives to this day the extraordinariness of the revelation of God.

Jesus, the Christ, the Saviour and God's Servant, is He who sets forth and reveals the mission of the nation Israel; He it is that fulfils the Covenant concluded between God and Abraham. When the Christian Church confesses Jesus Christ as Saviour and the Servant of God for us, for all men, also for the mighty majority of those who have no direct connexion with the people Israel, then it does not confess Him *although* He was a Jew (as if this 'Jewishness' in Jesus were a *pudendum*, which we had to ignore!). Nor can the view be that we believe in Jesus Christ, who was just an Israelite by accident, but who might quite as well have sprung from another nation. No, we must strictly consider that Jesus Christ, in whom we believe, whom we Christians out of the heathen call our Saviour and praise as the consummator of God's work on our behalf—He was *of necessity a Jew*. We cannot be blind to this fact; it belongs to the concrete reality of God's work and of His revelation. For Jesus Christ is the fulfilment of the covenant concluded by God with Abraham, Isaac and Jacob; and it is the reality of *this* covenant—not the idea of any covenant—which is the basis, the meaning and goal of creation, that is, of everything that is real in distinction from God. The problem of Israel is, since the problem of Christ is inseparable from it, the problem of existence as such. The man who is ashamed of Israel is ashamed of Jesus Christ and therefore of his own existence.

I have taken the topical illustration of the anti-Semitic core of National Socialism. It was no accidental matter, that we can regard lightheartedly, that here in Germany it was said that 'Judah is the enemy'. We may say this and in some circumstances we must say it; but let us be quite sure what we are doing. The attack on Judah means the attack on the rock of the work and revelation of God, beside which work and which revelation there is no other. The whole divine work and the whole divine revelation have been directly called in question, and not just in the realm of ideas and theories, but in the naturally historical realm, and so in the realm of temporal happening; called in question by what has taken place, by this fundamental anti-Semitism of the system so long predominant in Germany. It may perhaps be said that it *had* to come to such a collision; but in that case one must not be surprised that this collision ended as it did. A nation which—and that was the other side of National Socialism—chooses itself and makes itself the basis and measure of everything—such a nation *must* sooner or later collide with the truly chosen people of God. In the proclamation of the idea of such an elect nationality, even before anti-Semitism is expressed, there is already involved a basic denial of Israel and therewith a denial of Jesus Christ and therefore, finally, of God Himself. Anti-Semitism is the form of godlessness beside which, what is usually called atheism (as confessed say in Russia) is quite innocuous. For in anti-Semitic godlessness realities are involved irrespective of whether those who invented and worked this business were aware of them or not. Here what is involved is conflict with Christ. Theologically regarded—I am not at the moment speaking politically—this undertaking *had* to go to bits and break up. On this rock the assault of man is shattered, however powerfully undertaken. For the mission, the prophetic, priestly and kingly mission of the nation Israel is identical with God's will and work, as surely as it has been set forth and revealed in Jesus Christ.

What is the meaning of Israel's mission? When the Bible speaks of an election of Israel and of an unlikeness in this people to the other nations, when, that is, we apprehend in the Old Testament a special existence of Israel, what is thereby involved is a sending, a mission, an apostolate. What is involved in the existence of Israel is that a man appointed thereto by God is there in God's place on behalf of all other men. Such is Israel's reality, a man or a community, a people in God's service. Not for their own glory was this people picked out, not in the sense of a national claim, but for the other peoples and to that extent as the servant of all peoples. This people is God's commissioner. It has to proclaim His word; that is its prophetic mission. By its existence it has to be a witness that God not only speaks, but pledges Himself in person and surrenders Himself even unto death; that is its priestly mission. And, finally, in its political helplessness, it has as witness among the other nations to indicate the lordship of God over men; that is its kingly mission. Humanity needs this prophetic, priestly and kingly service. The Old Testament aims, in its complete reality, at making this mission of Israel visible, when again and again it expresses thankful praise of God for the miraculous succour and preservation of this tiny nation. In particular the prophetic mission of Israel is made visible in the emergence of definite persons, the prototype of whom, side by side with Abraham, is Moses, as the founder of Israel's national unity; and after him the prophets, who have constantly emerged in the most varied forms. A second line comes into view, in what is connected in the Old Testament with the tabernacle, the Temple and the sacrifices. And, thirdly, the kingly mission is once for all set forth in the kingdom of David, with its remarkable horizon in the kingdom of Solomon. It is in this kingdom of David that the goal of God's grace—Israel as representing God's sovereignty on earth—becomes visible as a type. But, finally—and this concerns us—this mission of Israel is fulfilled in the appearance and coming forward of the man Jesus of Nazareth out of this people, in His unquestionable belonging to this people.

Israel's mission must be understood as a mission fulfilled, revealed and accomplished in Jesus Christ. Hence it is in the first place hidden and ineffective. In fact, if we read the Old Testament as it speaks itself, then at the first glance, almost on every page, we can be convinced that it does not dream of exalting Israel as such, this nation or even 'race'. The picture which the Old Testament itself gives of the Israelite is in an utterly shattering way that of the man who *resists* his own election and consequently the mission given him, who proves himself unworthy and incapable of the mission, and who in consequence, since he is the object of God's grace, is continually struck down and broken by the judgment which afflicts him just because he withdraws from grace. What a problematic people this people Israel is in all stages of its history, is described by almost every book of the Old Testament. It goes from catastrophe to catastrophe, and always because it is disloyal to its God. This disloyalty is bound to mean damnation and destruction, as the prophets constantly indicate, or show as having already having happened. What is the upshot of this story? That prophecy in the end is dumb and only the dead written law survives. And what has become of the Temple and Israel's priesthood? Solomon's Temple, once the greatest hope of Israel, sinks into ruins and ashes. And what has become of Israel's kingship, the Kingdom of David? It is a grief for all Israelites, to think on what Israel once was, and what has now become of it under the strokes of God, who loved it so much and whose love was so ill requited. And when eventually the hope reaches fulfilment and the Messiah appears, Israel confirms its whole previous history in the Crucifixion. It confirms it by rejecting Him, not accidentally, but as blasphemers of God, and by banishing Him to the heathen and handing Him over to Pilate to be killed and hanged on the gallows. Such is Israel, this elect nation, which so deals with its own mission and election that it pronounces its own condemnation. The whole of anti-Semitism comes too late. The verdict has been pronounced long ago, and beside this verdict all other verdicts are puerile.

Is Israel's mission thereby superseded? No, on the contrary, through everything the Old Testament again and again insists that God's election holds and will hold to all eternity. This man who is thus set forth as he is in Israel, is and remains the man elect by God and the man in consequence entrusted with this mission. Where man fails, God's faithfulness triumphs. And this Israel, which is a great demonstration of man's unworthiness, at the same time becomes a demonstration of God's free grace, which asks no questions about man's attitude, but sovereignly pronounces upon man a 'nevertheless', by which he is upheld. Man is nothing but the object of the divine compassion, and where he wants to be more, he must necessarily rebel against this Israel-existence. Israel is simply thrown upon God and simply directed to Him. Read the Psalms: 'Thou only. . . .' Man appears simply as a hearer of God's Word, and is set, and remains, under God's lordship, even if he attempts time and again to withdraw from it. And in the fulfilment of his mission, in the crucified Jesus of Nazareth, here most of all it becomes visible once more what Israel means. What else is the Jesus hanging on the gallows but this Israel once more in its sin and godlessness? Yes, this blasphemer is Israel. And this Israel's name is now Jesus of Nazareth. And if we glance again at Jewish history and see the strangeness and absurdity of the Jew, his obnoxiousness which repeatedly made him odious among the nations—and now you may give the anti-Semitic register full play—what else does that mean but the confirmation of this rejected Israel, which by God was made visible at the Cross, but also of the Israel with whom God keeps faith right through all stages of his wandering? How do we know this? Because He kept faith with Israel on the

Cross of Golgotha. When was God nearer Israel than then? And where has God, by means of the nation Israel, stood more strongly and comfortingly beside all humanity than there? Do you believe that it lies with us to exclude the Jew from this faithfulness of God? Do you really believe that we can and may deny him this? God's faithfulness in the reality of Israel is in fact the guarantee of His faithfulness to us too, and to all men.

But now we must turn the page. Jesus Christ is the fulfilment, is the consummation of Israel. We look again into the Old Testament and find continual traces, that these obstinate and lost men—astoundingly enough!—in certain situations even confirm their election. When this occurs, when there is a kind of godly, upright continuity, this does not arise from the nature of Israel, but is rather God's ever renewed grace. But where there is grace, men are bound *contre cœur* to lift up their voice in praise of God, and bear witness that where God's light falls upon their life, a reflection of this light in them is bound to respond. There is a grace of God in the midst of judgment. And of this the Old Testament also speaks, not as of a continuity of Israelite man, but as of a 'nevertheless' of God. Nevertheless, there are in the history of this nation recurrent testimonies which begin with the words, 'Thus saith the Lord . . .' They sound out as the answer of such hearers, as the echo therefore of the 'nevertheless' of God's faithfulness. The Old Testament is aware of a 'remnant'. Here it is not the question of better or more moral men, but of those who are distinguished by having been called. Sinners gripped by God's grace, *peccatores justi*, are those who constitute the remnant.

Revelation culminates in the existence of Jesus of Nazareth. He comes out of Israel, born of Mary the Virgin, and yet from above, and so in His glory the Revealer and Consummator of the covenant. Israel is not a sick man who was allowed to recover, but One risen from the dead. By His appearing, over against the verdict that man pronounced on himself God's verdict comes into view, to remove all human self-condemnation. God's faithfulness triumphs in this sea of sin and misery. He has mercy on man. He shares with His inmost Being in this man. He has never ceased to lead by cords of love this people which to His face has behaved like a whore. It remains true that this man of Israel belongs to God and again and again, not by nature but by the miracle of grace, may belong anew to God, be rescued from death, be exalted to God's right hand.

Israel really is the presentation of God's free grace. So God becomes visible in relation to man, in the event in which Jesus Christ reaches the goal, in His resurrection from the dead. Here man appears surrounded by the light of the glory of God. That is grace, that is God's turning to man. And this becomes visible in the man out of Israel. In the train of this event—and once more grace is here positively visible—we arrive at that astounding extension of the covenant with Abraham, far beyond those who are of his blood: 'Go into all the world and proclaim the Gospel to every creature!' That is grace—from narrowness into spaciousness. Yet precisely because salvation is of the Jews, the Jewish nation is not only judged but also given grace. This reprieve of Israel, in the form of its election and calling which holds good unalterably, is to this day visible in the Church, which is in fact essentially a Church composed of Jews and heathen. In Romans 9–11 Paul lays the greatest stress on the fact that there is not a Church of the Jews and a Church of the heathen, but that the Church is the one community of those who come to faith out of Israel, together with those who are called out of the heathen to the Church. It is essential to the Christian Church to be both, and so far removed is it from having ever to be at any time ashamed of it, that it must realise that it is its title of honour, that the seed of Abraham lives in it also. The existence of Jewish Christians is the visible guarantee of the unity of the one people of God, which on its one side is called Israel and on its other the Church. Alongside the Church there is still a Synagogue, existing upon the denial of Jesus Christ and on a powerless continuation of Israelite history, which entered upon fullness long ago. But we have to remember that if it is God's will— and the Apostle Paul stood in puzzlement before this question —that this separated Israel still exists, we can only see the Synagogue as the shadow-picture of the Church, which accompanies it through the centuries, and, whether the Jews are aware of it or not, actually and really participates in the witness of God's revelation in the world. The good vine is not dried up. For that God planted it and what God has done to it and given to it, is the decisive thing; and it is made manifest in Jesus Christ, the man out of Israel.

12

GOD'S ONLY SON

God's revelation in the man Christ Jesus is compelling and exclusive and God's work in Him is helpful and adequate, because this man is not a being different from God, but the only Son of the Father; that is, God Himself uniquely living through and of Himself; He is God's omnipotence, grace and truth in person and therefore the authentic Mediator between God and all other men.

WE come to the question which is not a question because *a priori* the answer lies in the open—to the pronouncement of the true Deity of Jesus Christ. Let us try to make clear how we reach this pronouncement, or which is the question that leads to it.

Throughout our exposition we have come upon the concept of the revelation or the Word of God—that is, upon God's proclamation, the message that proceeds from Himself. There are all sorts of revelations and all sorts of words and messages, which have already reached men and are still reaching them, and which also raise the claim to be the Word and message of God. So the question arises—and we have to give our answer to it—how far what is here described as God's revelation is bound to be acknowledged and accepted as *the* revelation? There can be no doubt about it, that, by and large, in the history of humanity as a whole and in the life of every individual there are plenty of causes and opportunities, by which something or other becomes for us in a high degree illuminating, important and convincing, by which something 'overpowers' and imprisons us and draws us under its spell. Man's life alike in the microcosm as in the macrocosm is full of such experiences. There are 'revelations' of power and beauty and love in the life of men. Why then is just this, which is here termed God's revelation, the event that consists of the existence of Jesus Christ—why is it revelation in an emphatic, once-for-all way? The general answer to be given to this question (of the 'absoluteness' of Christianity, Troeltsch) is to this effect, that we admit that we are enveloped by other 'revelations', which carry a large degree of compulsion and rightly

82

make large claims. But starting from Christian faith we must say of these revelations, that they are lacking in a final, simply binding *authority*. We may traverse this world of revelations, we may be illumined here and convinced there and overpowered somewhere else; but they do not have the power of a first and last thing which would hinder man from enjoying and being intoxicated by such revelations, and then going on further, like a man who beholds his face in a mirror and passes on and forgets what he has seen. All these revelations are notoriously devoid of any final, binding force. Not because they are not powerful, not because they are not fraught with meaning and fascination, but because they are all concerned, as we are bound to maintain from the standpoint of the Christian faith, merely with revelations of the greatness, the power, the goodness, the beauty of the earth created by God. The earth is full of miracles and glory. It could not be God's *creature* and the area of our existence appointed us by God, if it were not full of revelations. The philosophers and the poets, the musicians and the prophets of all times are aware of it. But these revelations of the earth and the earthly spirit lack the authority which might bind man conclusively. Man may pass through this world without being ultimately bound. But there could also be *heavenly* revelations, that is, revelations of that invisible and inconceivable reality of creation, with which we are girt about. This world, too, of the impalpable and invisible is conceived in continuous movement towards us. Truly there are occasions of wonder there too. What would man be without meeting with heaven and the heavenly world? But neither do these heavenly revelations have the character of an ultimate authority; they too are in fact creaturely revelations. They too give no final answer. Everything heavenly, like everything earthly, is ultimately self-conditioned. It may meet us like the messenger of a great king, whom we might regard with astonishment as a great and mighty man, in face of whom, however, we still know that he is not the king himself; he is only his messenger. That is how we are situated over against all powers of heaven and earth and all their manifestations. We know that there is something higher. And however powerful these powers may be, though they may attain the enormity of an atom bomb, they do not ultimately compel us and therefore they do not ultimately impose upon us. 'Although the world collapse, 'tis but the ruins touch the fearless man.' Is it not the case that when we consider humanity and how it passed through these war years, did it not prove with astounding toughness, that all this did not affect it fundamentally? We have experienced the most frightful things, but man is not broken by the lords who are not the Lord. Intrepidly he passes through the ruins and asserts himself against the earthly powers.

When we in the Christian Church speak of revelation, we are not thinking of such earthly or heavenly revelations, but of the Power which is above all powers; not of the revelation of a divine Above or Below, but of the *revelation of God Himself*. That is why the Reality of which we are now speaking, God's revelation in Jesus Christ, is compelling and exclusive, helpful and adequate, because here we have not to do with a reality different from God, nor with one of those earthly or even heavenly realities, but with God Himself, with God in the highest, with the Creator of Heaven and earth, of whom we have heard in the first article. When in countless passages the New Testament speaks about Jesus of Nazareth as the Lord Jesus whom the Church recognises and confesses to be Jesus the Christ, it is using the same word which the Old Testament expresses by 'Jehovah'. This Jesus of Nazareth, who passes through the cities and villages of Galilee and wanders to Jerusalem, who is there accused and condemned and crucified, this man is the Jehovah of the Old Testament, is the Creator, is God Himself. A man like us in space and time, who has all the properties of God and yet does not cease to be a human being and a creature too. The Creator Himself, without encroaching upon His deity, becomes, not a demi-god, not an angel, but very soberly, very really a man. That is the meaning of the assertion of the Christian Confession about Jesus Christ, that He is God's only, or God's only-begotten Son. He is God's Son, and God in that sense of divine reality in which God is established by Himself. This God established by Himself, God's one Son, is *this man*, Jesus of Nazareth. Since God is not only the Father but also the Son, since in God's inner life this takes place continuously (He is God in the *act* of His Godness, He is Father *and* Son), He is capable of being the Creator, yet also the creature. This unheard-of 'yet also' has its inward analogy in the Father *and Son*. And since this work, this revelation of God, is the work of the eternal Son, it legitimately confronts the whole world of creatures, excellent beyond compare. Since here God Himself is involved, since this creature is His Son, the event in Jesus Christ is distinguished in truth as compelling and exclusive, as helpful and adequate above all else that happens round about us—though that too is by God's will and ordering. God's revelation and God's work in Jesus Christ is not any event on the basis of God's will, but is God Himself, who reaches utterance in the world of creatures.

We have now reached the point where I can let the text of the Confession of the early Church, proclaimed against the background of the discussions on the question of the divinity of Christ, speak to you: 'The only-begotten Son of God, begotten of his Father before all worlds, God of God, Light of Light, very God of very God, begotten not made, being of one substance with the Father, by whom all things were made: who for us men and our salvation came down from heaven' (Nicene Creed, A.D. 381). There have been many complaints and murmurings over this formula and probably, sooner or later in your studies, you will come up against men of letters and even teachers, who also do the same and think it dreadful that this matter should be reduced to this formula. I should be happy to think that, when you meet such complainers, this hour at college may come back to your memory and release a tiny check in you. This inveighing against so-called 'orthodoxy' is just a 'wolf's snarl', which an educated man should have nothing to do with. For there is something barbaric in this scolding at the Fathers. I should think, even if one is not a Christian, one should have enough respect to realise that the problem has been described here in a grand manner. It has been said of this Nicene formula that it is not found in that form in the Bible. But there is a great deal that is true and necessary and worth knowing, which is not word for word in the Bible. The Bible is not a letter-box but the grand document of the revelation of God. This revelation is meant to speak to us with a view to our grasping it ourselves. The Church has had at all times to answer what is said in the Bible. It has had to answer in other languages than Greek or Hebrew, in other words than those that stood there. Such an answer this formula is, which proved itself when the matter was attacked. There really *had* to be a tussle about the iota, whether this was God Himself or a heavenly or earthly being. That was not an indifferent question. In this iota the whole of the Gospel was at stake. Either in Jesus we have to do with God or with a creature. In the history of religion there have again and again been godlike beings. When

the old theology strove here unto blood, it was quite aware
why.

Frequently, of course, much that was simply human was added.
But that is not so momentous; even Christians are not angels.
Where a mighty matter is involved, we must not come along,
crying 'Quiet, quiet, dear little one'. But the strife must be
inexorably carried on to a finish. I should say, Thank God that
the Fathers at that time in all foolishness and weakness and with
all their Greek learning were not afraid to fight. In fact all the
formulae speak of just the one thing, the Only-begotten, begotten
of the Father before all time, the Son, Light of Light, very God
of very God, not a creature but God Himself, of *like* nature with
the Father, not just of similar nature, *God in Person.* 'By whom all
things were made and who for us men came down from heaven,
from above.' Down to us; this Person is Christ. In this way the
early Church saw Jesus Christ; in this way His reality confronted
it visibly, in this way it confessed Him in its Christian Confession,
which is a challenge to us, to try to see it so also. If a man understands it, why should he not unite his voice in the mighty con-
sensus of the Church? What childishness in view of this matter to
sigh over orthodoxy and Greek theology! That has nothing to do
with the matter. Even if at the outset there be a problematic
addition, let us admit that all we men do is problematic, shameful
and joyless, and that things must still go on running their course,
that they issue as is necessary and right. *Dei providentia et hominum
confusione!*—In this Confession the point involved is quite simple
and practical, that we may be certain of what we are after,
namely, that in this confession of the Son of God the Christian
faith is in fact distinguished from all that bears the name of
religion. We have to do with God Himself, not with any gods. In
Christian faith we have to do with 'becoming partakers of the
divine nature'. Actually nothing more or less is involved than that
the divine nature itself has come nigh unto us and that in faith
we become partakers of it, according as it meets us in the One.
In this way Jesus Christ is the Mediator between God and man.
Everything must be understood against this background. Less
than this God did not will to do for us. We may realise the utter
depth of our human sin and need in the fact that this immeasurable thing had to happen and did happen. The Church and all
Christendom looks in its message at this immeasurable and
unfathomable fact, that God has given Himself for us. And that

do justice to it is another question. We have to be told that it has been taken. This decision has nothing to do with a destiny, a neutral and objective determination of man, which could somehow be read off from man's nature or history; but this sovereign decision on the existence of every man consists in the existence of the man Jesus Christ. Because He is and was and will be, this sovereign decision is imposed upon all men. You remember that at the beginning of our lectures, as we were expounding the concept of faith, we decided that Christian faith must be regarded absolutely as a man's decision, which is made in view of a divine decision. At this point we now see the concrete form of this divine decision. When we say that God is our Lord and Master, we Christians are not thinking, after the fashion of all mysticism, of an indefinable and ultimately unknown divine somewhat, which stands over us as a power and dominates us. But we are thinking of this concrete figure, the man Jesus Christ. He is our Lord. Because He exists, God is our Lord. In precedence of all human existence, as the *a priori*, goes the existence of Jesus Christ. That is what the Christian Confession of faith says. What is meant by this precedence of His? Do not let the idea of a temporal precedence be prominent. That is also there, for it is finished, there is that great historical perfect, in which lordship was set up over us, in the years 1–30 in Palestine—but that is not the decisive thing. When the temporal precedence acquires this importance, that is because the existence of this man precedes our existence in virtue of His incomparable *worth*. He precedes our existence in virtue of His authority over our existence, in the power of His divinity. We look back on what we were saying in the last lecture. We can now see what was meant when we said that the existence of this man is, quite simply, the existence of God Himself. That is what constitutes the value of this man, that is the content of His life, that is His power over us. Because Jesus Christ is God's only begotten Son, 'of one substance with the Father', therefore His human nature too, His human being, is an event in which sovereign decision is consummated. His humanity is humanity indeed, the essence of all *humanitas*. Not as a concept or an idea, but as a decision, as history. Jesus Christ is *the* man, and the measure, the determination and limitation of all human being. He is the decision as to what God's purpose and what God's goal is, not just for Him but for every man. It is in this sense that the Christian Confession calls Jesus Christ 'our Lord'.

This sovereign, kingly decision in Jesus Christ is grounded on the fact that by God's disposal this one man stands for all. It is grounded, that is, this sovereign decision of God—namely, the lordship of Jesus Christ—is not a blind act of power in itself towards us men. You remember how we spoke of God's almightiness and how I underlined the statement that 'power in itself' is evil; that power for power's sake is the Devil. The lordship of Jesus Christ is not power for power's sake. And when the Christian Church confesses that 'I believe that Jesus Christ is my Lord', then it is not thinking of a blind law standing threateningly over us, not of an historical power, not of a destiny or fate to which man is exposed defenceless, in face of which his final insight could only consist in acknowledging it as such; but it is thinking of the proper lordship of its Lord. His lordship is not only *potentia*; it is *potestas*. It becomes recognisable to us as the ordering not simply of an unsearchable will, but as the *ordering of wisdom*. God is right and God knows why He does so, if He is our Lord and wills to be known and acknowledged by us as such. Of course, this basis of Christ's lordship leads us into mystery. Here is something objective, an order which is set high above us and apart from us, an order to which man must subject himself, which he must acknowledge, of which he can only hear, and must be obedient to it. How could it be otherwise, since the very lordship of Christ has been set up and consists in the power of His Godhead? Where God is king, man can but fall down and adore. But adore in presence of the wisdom of God, of His righteousness and holiness, of the mystery of His mercy. That is Christian reverence before God and Christian praise of God, Christian service and obedience. Obedience rests upon hearing, and hearing means receiving a word.

I should like to try and indicate this basis of Christ's lordship quite shortly and concisely. The opening statement says that this sovereign decision is based on the fact, that this One by God's dispensation stands for all. The mystery of God, and thus also of Jesus Christ, is that He, this One, this man, by His being One—not an idea, but One who is quite concrete at that time and place, a man who bears a name and comes from a place, who like us all has a life-history in time—not only exists for Himself but is this One for all. You must try to read the New Testament from the standpoint of this 'for us'. For the entire existence of this man, who stands in the centre, is determined by the fact that it is a human existence, achieved and accomplished not only in its own framework and with its own meaning in itself, but for all others. In this one man God sees every man, all of us, as through a glass. Through this medium, through this *Mediator* we are known and seen by God. And we may, and should, understand ourselves as men seen by God in Him, in this man, as men made known to Him in this way. Before His eyes from eternity God keeps men, each man, in Him, in this One; and not only before His eyes but loved and elect and called and made His possession. In Him He has from eternity bound Himself to each, to all. Along the entire line it holds, from the creatureliness of man, through the misery of man, to the glory promised to man. Everything is decided about us in Him, in this one man. It is the likeness of this One, the likeness of God, after which man has been created man. This One in His humiliation bears the sin, the wickedness and folly, and the misery and the death of all. And the glory of this One is the glory that is intended for us all. For us it is intended that we may serve Him in eternal righteousness, innocence and blessedness, even as He has risen from death, lives and rules in eternity. Such is God's wise dispensation, this cohesion of each man and all men with this One. And that is, seen so to speak from above, the basis of the lordship of Jesus Christ.

And now the same thing seen from man's side. Since this dispensation of God's exists, since we are set in this cohesion, since Jesus Christ is this one man and stands before God on our behalf, and we in Him are loved, upheld, led and borne by God, we are Jesus Christ's property, we are bound in duty to Him, this Proprietor. Note well that this appointment of us to be His property, this connexion from us to Him does not possess in the first instance anything like a moral or even a religious quality, but it rests upon a state of affairs, upon an objective order. The moral and religious element is a *cura posterior*. Of course the result will necessarily also include an element of morality and religion. But in the first instance the fact is simply that we belong to Him. In virtue of God's dispensation man is Christ's property, not in spite of but in his freedom. For what man knows and lives as his freedom, he lives in the freedom which is given him and created for him by the fact that Christ intercedes for him in the presence of God. That is the great good action of God, signified in this, that Jesus Christ is the Lord. It is the divineness of this good action, the divineness of the everlasting mercy

which, before we existed or thought of Him, has sought and found
us in Him. It is this divine mercy which is also for us the basis of
Christ's lordship and which delivers us from all other lordships.
It is this divine mercy which excludes the right of all other lords
to speak and makes it impossible to set up another authority
alongside this authority and another lord alongside this Lord
and to hearken to him. And it is this eternal mercy, in which this
dispensation over us is included, which makes it impossible to
appeal past the Lord Jesus Christ to another lord and to reckon
once more with fate or history or nature, as though these were
what really dominated us. Once we have seen that Christ's
potestas is based on God's mercy, goodness and love, only then
do we abandon all reservations. Then the division into a religious
sphere and other spheres falls out. Then we cease to separate
between body and soul, between service of God and politics. All
these separations cease, for man is one, and as such is subject to
the lordship of Christ.

The community knows that Jesus Christ is our Lord, it is
known in the Church. But the truth of 'our Lord' does not depend
on our knowing or acknowledging it or on the existence of a
congregation where it is discerned and expressed; it is because
Jesus Christ is our Lord that He can be known and proclaimed
as such. But no one knows as a matter of course that all men have
their Lord in Him. This knowledge is a matter of our election and
calling, a matter of the community gathered together by His
word, a matter of the Church.

I have quoted Luther's exposition of the second article.
One might raise against this exposition the objection, that
Luther has made of the 'our' Lord a 'my' Lord. I would
not, of course, venture to make of this a reproach against
Luther; for by this concentration upon the individual Luther's
exposition acquires a quite extraordinary weight and urgency.
'*My* Lord!'—by that the whole achieves an unheard-of actuality
and existentiality. But we must not lose sight of the fact that, in
agreement with the usual expression of the New Testament, the
Confession says '*our* Lord'. Just as in the Lord's Prayer we pray
in the plural, not as a crowd but as a fellowship. The confession
'our Lord' is the confession of those who are called in His congregation to be brothers and sisters, with a general commission to
face the world. It is they who know and confess Jesus Christ as the
person He is. They call Him 'our' Lord. But once we are clear that

there is such a place of knowledge and confession, we must look outwards again at the broad scene; and we must not regard the 'our Lord' in any restricted sense, as though the Christian congregation had their Lord in Jesus Christ, but other assemblies and communities had other lords. The New Testament has left no doubt as to the fact that there is only one Lord and that this Lord is the Lord of the world, Jesus Christ. This is what the community has to preach to the world. The truth and reality of the Church belong to the third article. But this much may already be said here, that the community of Jesus Christ is not a reality which exists for its own sake; it exists because it has a commission. What it knows it has to tell the world. 'Let your light shine before men.' By doing this, by being just as it was from the beginning, the unique, living advertisement over against the world, the advertisement of the existence of the Lord, it thus raises no false claim for itself, for its faith and its knowledge. No, Jesus Christ is the Lord.

Here too therefore the Nicene Creed has a good little expansion compared with the Apostles' Creed—namely, *unicum dominum*, the *sole* Lord. To express and to advertise *this* is the Church's commission. Among Christians and in the congregation we ought to regard what is called the 'world', as *a priori* nothing else than the realm, than those men, who ought to get to hear this very thing, and moreover from *us*. Everything else that we fancy we know about the world, all the statements of its godlessness are secondary propositions and do not concern us fundamentally. What interests and concerns us Christians is not that the world does not stand where we stand, that it closes its heart and its head to faith, but merely that it, that these men are the people who ought to get to *hear* it from us, to whom we may advertise the Lord.

At this point I should like, in passing, to answer a question which has been put to me several times during these weeks: 'Are you not aware that many are sitting in this class who are not Christians?' I have always laughed and said: 'That makes no difference to me.' It would be quite dreadful if the faith of Christians should aim at sundering and separating one man from the others. It is in fact the strongest motive for collecting men and binding them together. And what binds is, quite simply and challengingly, at the same time the commission which the community has to deliver its message. If we consider the matter once more from the standpoint of the community, that is, from the standpoint of those who seriously wish to be Christians—'Lord, I believe: help Thou mine unbelief!'—we must remember that everything will depend upon the Christians not painting for the non-Christians in word and deed a *picture* of the Lord or an *idea* of Christ, but on their succeeding with their human words and ideas in pointing to Christ Himself. For it is not the conception of Him, not the dogma of Christ that is the real Lord, but He who is attested in the word of the Apostles. Be it said to those who account themselves believers: May it be given us not to set up an image, when we speak of Christ, a Christian idol, but in all our weakness to point to Him who is the Lord and so, in the power of His Godhead, the sovereign decision upon the existence of *every* man.

14

THE MYSTERY AND THE MIRACLE
OF CHRISTMAS

*The truth of the conception of Jesus Christ by the Holy Spirit and
of His birth of the Virgin Mary points to the true Incarnation of
the true God achieved in His historical manifestation, and recalls
the special form through which this beginning of the divine act of
grace and revelation, that occurred in Jesus Christ, was distinguished
from other human events.*

WE have now come to one of the places, and perhaps indeed
to *the* place, at which at all times, and even largely within
the Christian community, offence has been taken. And perhaps
it is your experience too, that you were ready to follow the
explanation so far, although now and then with an uneasy feeling,
as to where this is going to lead next; and that you are brought
up short by what is coming now—and which is not my invention but the Confession of the Church! We don't want to become
anxious, but having gone so far on our way in comparative
peace, we want to approach this section also just as peacefully
and objectively, the section 'conceived by the Holy Spirit, born
of the Virgin Mary'. Here too our concern must be simply with
the truth; but we also wish to draw near reverently, so that the
anxious question, *Must* we believe this? is not the last thing, but
that perhaps even here we may joyfully say Yes.

We have to do with the beginning of a whole series of pronouncements about Jesus Christ. What we have been hearing so
far was the description of the subject. Now we listen to a number
of definitions—conceived, born, suffered, crucified, buried,
descended, rose again, seated on the right hand of God, from
thence He shall come again . . . which describe an action or an
event. We are concerned with the story of a life, starting with
generation and birth like any human life; and then a life-work
remarkably compressed into the little word 'suffered', a passion-
story, and finally the divine confirmation of this life in its Resurrection, its Ascension, and the still outstanding conclusion, that

from thence He shall come to judge the quick and the dead. He who acts and lives is Jesus Christ, God's only Son, our Lord.

If we wish to understand the meaning of 'conceived by the Holy Ghost and born of the Virgin Mary', above all we must try to see that these two remarkable pronouncements assert that God of free grace became man, a real man. The eternal Word became flesh. This is the miracle of Jesus Christ's existence, this descent of God from above downwards—the Holy Ghost and the Virgin Mary. This is the mystery of Christmas, of the Incarnation. At this part of the Confession the Catholic Church makes the sign of the Cross. And in the most various settings composers have attempted to reproduce this *et incarnatus est*. This miracle we celebrate annually, when we celebrate Christmas.

> *If I to grasp this miracle should will,*
> *So stands my spirit reverently still.*

Such *in nuce* is God's revelation; we can only grasp it, only hear it as the beginning of all things.

But there is no question here of conception and birth in general, but of a quite definite conception and a quite definite birth. Why conception by the Holy Spirit and why birth of the Virgin Mary? Why this special miracle which is intended to be expressed in these two concepts, side by side with the great miracle of the Incarnation? Why does the miracle of Christmas run parallel to the mystery of the Incarnation? A noetic utterance is so to speak put alongside the ontic one. If in the Incarnation we have to do with the thing, here we have to do with the sign. The two should not be confused. The thing which is involved in Christmas is true in and for itself. But it is indicated, it is unveiled in the miracle of Christmas. But it would be wrong to conclude from that, that therefore 'only' a sign is involved, which therefore might even be deducted from the mystery. Let me warn you against this. It is rare in life to be able to separate form and content.

'Very God and very man.' If we consider this basic Christian truth first in the light of 'conceived by the Holy Spirit', the truth is clear that the man Jesus Christ has His origin simply in God, that is, He owes His beginning in history to the fact that God in person became man. That means that Jesus Christ is indeed man, true man, but He is not just a man, not just an extra-ordinarily gifted or specially guided man, let alone a super-man;

but, while being a man, He is God Himself. God is one with Him. His existence begins with God's special action; as a man He is founded in God, He is true God. The subject of the story of Jesus Christ is therefore God Himself, as truly as a man lives and suffers and acts there. And as surely as human initiative is involved in this life, so surely this human initiative has its foundation in the fact that in Him and through Him God has taken the initiative. From this standpoint we cannot avoid saying that Jesus Christ's Incarnation is an analogue of creation. Once more God acts as the Creator, but now not as the Creator out of nothing; rather, God enters the field and creates within creation a new beginning, a new beginning in history and moreover in the history of Israel. In the continuity of human history a point becomes visible at which God Himself hastens to the creature's aid and becomes one with him. God becomes man. In this way this story begins.

And now we have to turn the page and come to the second thing expressed thereby, when we say, 'born of the Virgin Mary'. Now the fact is underlined that we are on earth. There is a human child, the Virgin Mary; and as well as coming from God, Jesus also comes from this human being. God gives Himself an earthly human origin, that is the meaning of 'born of Mary the Virgin'. Jesus Christ is not 'only' true God; that would not be real incarnation—but neither is He an intermediate being; He is a man like us all, a man without reservation. He not only resembles us men; He is the same as us. As God is the Subject in the life of Jesus Christ, so man is the object in this story, but in the sense not of an object to be acted upon, but of a man who is in action. Man does not turn into a marionette in this meeting with God, but if there is genuine humanity, here it is, where God Himself makes Himself a man.

That would constitute the one circle which is to be seen here; namely true divinity and true humanity in sheer unity. In the Council of Chalcedon, 451, the Church attempted to rail off this unity against all misunderstandings; against the Monophysite unification, which resulted in so-called Docetism, which is fundamentally unaware of any true humanity in Christ—God only apparently became man—and against the Nestorian attempt to widen the gap between God and man, which simply wanted to separate, and according to which the Deity of Christ can be thought of every minute as separated from His humanity. Moreover, this doctrine goes back to an older error, that of the so-called Ebionites. From these Ebionites the way led to the Arians, who wished to understand Christ merely as a specially exalted creature. The Council of Chalcedon formulated the thesis that the unity is 'without confusion, without change, without division, without separation'. Perhaps you are inclined to describe this as a 'theologians' foundling' or as a 'parsons' quarrel'. Yet in all such squabbles the concern has never been to set the mystery aside, as though we wanted by such formulae to solve the matter rationistically; but the early Church's endeavour was—and that is why it is still worth while to listen to it—to lead the eyes of Christians in the proper way to this mystery. All other attempts were attempts to resolve the mystery into a human comprehensibility. God for Himself and a mysterious man, that can be grasped; and even the unique coincidence of this God and this man in the form of Jesus can be explained. But these theories, against which the Early Church turns, do not regard the mystery. But the early Orthodox were concerned to gather men about this centre, that the man who refuses to believe should leave it alone; but nothing must be watered down here; this salt must not lose its savour. Hence the great expenditure of effort by the early Councils and theologians. It is always a little plebeian of us nowadays, out of our on the whole somewhat barbaric intellectuality, to say that they went 'too far' in those days, instead of being grateful for the fundamental work that was done then. You need not, of course, mount the pulpit and recite these formulae; but you should take the matter as quite fundamental. Christendom has seen and fixed what is involved in the miracle of Christmas, namely, the *unio hypostatica*, the genuine unity of true God and true man in the one Jesus Christ. And we are challenged to hold on to it.

But now all of you certainly notice, that in these expressions 'conceived by the Holy Spirit' and 'born of the Virgin Mary' something special is still being expressed. The talk is of an unusual procreation and an unusual birth. This thing is called the *nativitas Jesu Christi*. A miracle points to the mystery of the true divinity and the true humanity, the miracle of this procreation and of this birth.

What is the meaning of 'conceived by the Holy Spirit'? It does not mean that the Holy Spirit is so to speak the Father of Jesus Christ; in the strict sense only the denial is thereby asserted, that the man Jesus Christ has no Father. At His procreation it was not as when a human existence starts, but this human existence starts in the freedom of God Himself, in the freedom in which the Father and Son are one in the bond of love, in the Holy Spirit. So when we look at the beginning of the existence of Jesus, we are meant to be looking into this ultimate depth of the Godhead, in which the Father and Son are one. This is the freedom of the inner life of God, and in this freedom the existence of this man begins in A.D. 1. By this taking place, by God Himself beginning quite concretely at this point with Himself, this man who of himself is neither capable of this nor willing, may not only proclaim the Word of God, but Himself be the Word of God. In the midst of the old the new humanity begins. This is the miracle of Christmas, the miracle of the procreation of Jesus Christ without a father. This has nothing to do with myths narrated elsewhere in the history of religion, myths of the procreation of men by gods. We have not to do with such a procreation here. God Himself takes the stage as the Creator and not as a partner to this Virgin. Christian art in earlier times attempted to reproduce this fact, that here there is no question of a sexual event. And it has been well said that this procreation was realised rather by way of the ear of Mary, which heard the Word of God.

'Born of the Virgin Mary.' Once again and now from the human standpoint the male is excluded here. The male has nothing to do with this birth. What is involved here is, if you like, a divine act of judgment. To what is to begin here man is to contribute nothing by his action and initiative. Man is not simply excluded, for the Virgin is there. But the male, as the specific agent of human action and history, with his responsibility for directing the human species, must now retire into the background, as the powerless figure of Joseph. That is the Christian reply to the question of woman: here the woman stands absolutely in the foreground, moreover the *virgo*, the Virgin Mary. God did not choose man in his pride and in his defiance, but man in his weakness and humility, not man in his historical rôle, but man in the weakness of his nature as represented by the woman, the human creature who can confront God only with the words, 'Behold, the handmaid of the Lord; be it unto me according as Thou hast said'. Such is human co-operation in this matter, that and only that! We must not think of making a merit of this handmaid existence, nor attempt once more to ascribe a potency to the creature. But God has regarded man in his weakness and in his humility, and Mary has expressed what creation alone can express in this encounter. That Mary does so and that thereby the creature says 'Yes' to God, is a part of the great acceptance which comes to man from God.

The miracle of Christmas is the actual form of the mystery of the personal union of God and man, the *unio hypostatica*. Again and again the Christian Church and its theology has insisted that we cannot postulate that the reality of the Incarnation, the mystery of Christmas, had by absolute necessity to take the form of this miracle. The true Godhead and the true humanity of Jesus Christ in their unity do not depend on the fact that Christ was conceived by the Holy Spirit and born of the Virgin Mary. All that we can say is that it pleased God to let the mystery be real and become manifest in this shape and form. But again that cannot mean that over against this factual form of the miracle we are as it were free to affirm it or not to affirm it, to make a deduction and say that we have listened, but make a reservation, that this matter could be also in another form for us. We perhaps best understand the relation of matter and form, which is presented here, by taking a look at the story, familiar to you all, of the healing of the paralytic (Mark 2. 10): 'That ye may know, that the Son of Man hath power to forgive sins. . . . Arise, take up thy bed and go thy way.' 'That ye may know . . .'; in this way the miracle of the Virgin Birth is also to be understood. What is involved is the mystery of the Incarnation as the visible form of which the miracle takes place. We should ill have understood Mark 2, if we wanted so to read the passage, that the chief miracle was the forgiveness of sins, and the bodily healing incidental. The one thing obviously belongs of necessity to the other. And so we should have to give a warning, too, against parenthesising the miracle of the *nativitas* and wanting to cling to the mystery as such. One thing may be definitely said, that every time people want to fly from this miracle, a theology is at work, which has ceased to understand and honour the mystery as well, and has rather essayed to conjure away the mystery of the unity of God and man in Jesus Christ, the mystery of God's free grace. And on the other hand, where this mystery has been understood and men have avoided any attempt at natural theology, because they had no need of it, the miracle came to be thankfully and joyously recognised. It became, we might say, an inward necessity at this point.

15

SUFFERED . . .

The life of Jesus Christ is not a triumph but a humiliation, not a success but a failure, not a joy but suffering. For that very reason it reveals man's rebellion against God and God's wrath against man which necessarily follows; but it also reveals the mercy in which God has made His own man's business and consequently his humiliation, failure and suffering, so that it need no longer be man's business.

IN Calvin's Catechism we may on this passage read the extra-ordinary conclusion that in the Confession the life of Jesus has been passed over up to the Passion, because what took place in this life up to the Passion does not belong to the 'substance of our redemption'. I take the liberty of saying that here Calvin is wrong. How can anyone say that the rest of Jesus' life is not substantially for our redemption? In that case what would be its significance? A mere superfluous narrative? I should think that there is involved in the *whole* of Jesus' life the thing that takes its beginning in the article 'He suffered'. In Calvin we have a delightful example before our eyes, of pupils of a great master often seeing better than he; for in the Heidelberg Catechism, composed by Calvin's pupils, Olevian and Ursin, Question 37 asks: 'What understandest thou by the little word "suffered"?' 'That He *all the time of His life on earth,* but especially at the end thereof, hath borne in body and soul the wrath of God against the sin of the whole human race.' For Calvin's view it might, of course, be adduced that Paul, and the Epistles of the New Testament in general, scarcely refer to this 'whole time' of Christ's life, and that the Apostles also, according to Acts, seem to have shown remarkably little interest in the matter. For them apparently only the one thing stands out, that, betrayed by the Jews, He was delivered to the Gentiles, was crucified and rose from the dead. But if the early Christian Church has so fully concentrated its gaze upon the Crucified and Risen One, that is not to be taken exclusively, but inclusively. The fact that Christ died and rose again is a reduction of the *whole* life of Jesus; but in that we must also see its development. The whole life of Jesus comes under the heading 'suffered'.

That is an extremely astonishing fact, for which we have not been straightway prepared by what has been said. Jesus Christ, God's only Son, our Lord, conceived by the Holy Spirit, born of the Virgin Mary, true Son of God and true son of man—what is the relation to that of the unfolding of His whole life under the sign of His having 'suffered'? We should expect something different, something resplendent, triumphant, successful, joyful. And as it is, we hear not a word of that, but, predominant for the entirety of this life, the assertion that 'He suffered'. Is that really the last word? We cannot overlook how this whole life ends: the third day He rose again from the dead. And the life of Jesus is not completely without sign of the coming joy and the coming victory. Not for nothing is there so much talk of glorification, and not for nothing is the picture of wedding joy so often mentioned. Although it is certainly not without amazement that we several times hear of Jesus weeping, but never that He laughed, it has still to be said that continuously through His suffering there was a kind of glint of joy in nature around Him, in children, and above all, of joy in His existence and in His mission. We hear once that it is said that He rejoiced over the fact that God had hidden it from the wise, but had revealed it unto the babes. And in the miracles of Jesus there is triumph and joy. Healing and help here break into the life of men. It seems to become visible who is in action. In the story of the Transfiguration, in which it is related that the disciples saw Jesus whiter than any white which is terrestrially possible, this other thing, the issue of this life—we might also say, its beginning and origin—becomes visible by anticipation. Bengel is undoubtedly right when he says of the Gospels before the Resurrection that we might say of all those stories of Jesus that they *spirant resurrectionem*. But more than that we cannot actually say. There is a fragrance of the beginning and of the end, a fragrance of the triumphant Deity who is in action there.

But the present time of His life is really suffering from the start. There is no doubt that for the Evangelists Luke and Matthew the childhood of Jesus, His Birth in the stable of Bethlehem, were already under the sign of suffering. This man is persecuted all His life, a stranger in His own family—what shocking statements He can make!—and in His nation; a stranger in the spheres of State and Church and civilisation. And what a road of manifest ill-success He treads! In what utter loneliness and temptation He stands among men, the leaders of His nation, even over against the masses of the people and in the very circle of His disciples! In this narrowest circle He is to find His betrayer; and in the man to whom He says, 'Thou art the Rock . . .', the man who denies Him thrice. And, finally, it is the disciples of whom it is said that 'they all forsook Him'. And the people cry in chorus, 'Away with him! Crucify him!' The entire life of Jesus is lived in this loneliness and thus already in the shadow of the Cross. And if the light of the Resurrection lights up here and there, that is the exception that proves the rule. The son of man *must* go up unto Jerusalem, must there be condemned, scourged and crucified—to rise again the third day. But first it is this dominant 'must' which leads him to the gallows.

What does it mean? Is it not the opposite of what we might expect from the news that God became Man? Here there is suffering. Notice that it is here for the first time in the Confession that the great problem of evil and suffering meets us directly. Already, of course, we have frequently had to refer to it. But according to the letter this is the first time we have an indication of the fact that in the relation between Creator and creature every-thing is not at its best, that lawlessness and destruction hold sway, that pain is added and suffered. Here for the first time the shadowy side of existence enters into our field of view, and not in the first article, which speaks of God the Creator. Not in the description of creation as heaven and earth, but here in the description of the existence of the Creator become creature, evil appears; here afar off death also becomes visible. The fact that this is so at least means this: that discretion is demanded in all descriptions of wickedness and evil as being to some extent independent. When that was done later, it was more or less overlooked that all this enters the field only in connexion with Jesus Christ. He has suffered, He has rendered visible what the nature of evil is, of man's revolt against God. What do we know of evil and sin? What do we know of what is called suffering or what death means? Here we get to know it. Here appears this complete darkness in its reality and truth. Here complaint is raised and punished, here the relation between God and man is really made clear. What are all our sighs, what is all that man thinks he knows about his folly and sinfulness and about the lost state of the world, what is all speculation about suffering and death beside what becomes manifest here? He, He has suffered, who is true God and true man. All independent talk on the subject—that is, talk cut loose from Him—will necessarily be inadequate and imperfect. Unless talk on this matter goes out from this centre, it will be unreal. That man can bear the most frightful strokes of Fate and comes through untouched by anything as through a shower of rain: that can be seen by us to-day. We are simply untouched either by suffering or by evil in its proper reality; we know that now. So we can repeatedly escape from the knowledge of our guilt and sin. We can only achieve proper knowledge, when we know that He who is true God and true man has suffered. In other words, it needs faith to see what suffering is. *Here* there was suffering. Everything else that we know as suffering is unreal suffering compared with what has happened here. Only from this stand-point, by sharing in the suffering He suffered, can we recognise the fact and the cause of suffering everywhere in the creaturely cosmos, secretly and openly.

If we look at this 'He suffered', we must begin from the fact that it was *God* who became man in Jesus Christ, who now had to suffer, not from the imperfection of the creaturely world, not from any pattern of nature, but from men and from their attitude to Him. From Bethlehem to the Cross He was abandoned by the world that surrounded Him, repudiated, persecuted, finally accused, condemned and crucified. Such is man's attack upon Him, upon God Himself. Here there is an unveiling of man's rebellion against God. God's Son is denied and rejected. With God's Son men can only do what they did according to the parable of the wicked vine-dressers: 'Here comes the Son and Heir, let us kill Him and take his inheritance for ourselves.' Such is man's answer to the gracious presence of God. To His grace, he has but a hate-filled 'No' to utter. It is the nation of Israel which rejects in Jesus its Messiah and King. It is the nation of Israel, with the promised Leader of its entire history, to which He gives meaning, concludes and fulfils it, which knows nothing better than to deliver Him finally to the heathen to be put to death. Jesus dies the penal death of Roman justice, as one de-livered up by Israel to the heathen. So Israel deals with its Saviour. And the heathen world in the form of Pilate can for its part only accept this handing over. It executes the judgment which the Jews have pronounced, and thereby participates likewise in this rebellion against God. What Israel does here is the revelation of a content which was present in the entire history of Israel: the men sent by God are not received joyfully as helpers, comforters and healers, but from Moses onwards, and here once again, conclusively, they are met by the fact that man says *No* to them. This *No* directly touches God Himself. Thus only in this ultimate, most intimate and direct presence of God does the utter remoteness of man from Him become manifest. Here it becomes manifest what sin is. Sin means to reject the grace of God as such, which approaches us and is present to us. Israel thinks it is able to help itself. Seen from this point, we must say that all we think we know as sin is petty and incidental and a mere application of this original sin. Just as in the Old Testament all commandments have but the one intention, of binding the people of Israel into God's covenant of grace, so the transgression of all commandments is wicked and bad, because it manifests man's protest against God's grace. The fact that Jesus the Son of God has suffered under Jews and heathen reveals—and it alone does reveal—evil in its reality. From this point alone can we grasp the fact, the extent, and the content of the impeachment of man. For the first time we are faced here with the root of all great and petty transgressions. So long as in all our sinning and our mutual guilt in great and petty ways we do not recognise this root and see ourselves accused in Christ's suffering, see ourselves again in that rebellion of man against God Himself, all knowledge or recognition of guilt is vain. For all knowledge of guilt apart from *this* knowledge we can get rid of again, like a poodle that has got wet, which shakes itself and trots on. So long as we have not yet seen wickedness in its real nature, we are not arrested (even if we speak in strong words of our guilt) into confessing, 'I have sinned against heaven and in Thy sight'. This 'in Thy sight' becomes obvious here, and obvious as the core and meaning of all the individual guilt in which we are involved. This individual guilt does not thereby become incidental. What is done by men in individual actions, from the action of Pilate down to that of Judas, is the rejection of the grace of God. But what is there done by men acquires its whole importance from its being done to God. For our knowledge of evil everything will depend on our recognising that man is under the accusation of being the offender against God. We can only see the infinite guilt in which we stand over against God; the God who became

man. Where we are guilty towards man, we are automatically
reminded of *this* man. For every man whom we have offended and
tormented is one of those whom Jesus Christ has called His
brethren. Now what we have done to Him, we have done to God.

It is true that in Jesus' life and in the story of His Passion
it is also simply the life of a man which unrolls. Think of
the great works of Christian art, of Grünewald's vision of the
Sufferer on the Cross, down to the less gifted attempts, in the
so-called 'ways of the Passion' of Catholic piety: all this is the
Man in His torment, as He sinks down by degrees into the straits
of tribulation, of being smitten, and finally of death. But even
regarded from this aspect it is not just man in his imperfection
who as a mortal being must be tormented through not being God;
for the figure of the suffering Jesus is the figure of one condemned
and punished. From the very start, what causes Jesus' suffering
is the legal action of His nation, which finally becomes quite
explicit. They see in Him the alleged Messiah who is different from
the one expected by them, against whose claim they can therefore
only protest. Think of the attitude of the Pharisees, right up to the
Sanhedrin: there you have the pronouncement of a verdict. This
verdict is laid before the worldly judge and executed by Pilate.
The Gospels have laid emphasis precisely upon this legal act.
Jesus is the Person accused, condemned and punished. Here in
this legal action is disclosed man's rebellion against God.

But in it there is also disclosed the wrath of God against
man. 'Suffered' is explained in the Heidelberg Catechism as
that Jesus has borne the wrath of God His whole life. Being
a man means being so placed before God as to have deserved
this wrath. In this unity of God and man the man is bound to
be this condemned and smitten person. The man Jesus in His
unity with God is the figure of man smitten by God. Even
this world's justice, which carries out this judgment, does so by
God's will. God's Son became man in order to let man be seen
under God's wrath. The Son of man *must* suffer and be delivered
up and crucified, says the New Testament. In this Passion the
connexion becomes visible between infinite guilt and the reconciliation that necessarily ensues upon this guilt. It becomes clear
that where God's grace is rejected, man rushes into his own mischief. It is here, where God Himself has become man, that the
deepest truth of human life is manifest: the total suffering which
corresponds to total sin.

To be a man means to be so situated in God's presence as Jesus is, that is, to be the Bearer of the wrath of God. It belongs to us, that end on the gallows. Yet that is not the final thing, neither man's rebellion nor God's wrath. But the deepest mystery of God is this, that God Himself in the man Jesus does not avoid taking the place of sinful man and being (He hath made Him to be sin, who knew no sin) that which man is, a rebel, and bearing the suffering of such a one, to be Himself the entire guilt and the entire reconciliation! That is what God has done in Jesus Christ. This is, to be sure, the utterly hidden element in this life, which first sees the light in the resurrection of Christ. But Christ's passion would be ill interpreted, if we were to go no further than the complaint about man and his lot. In truth, the suffering of Christ is not exhausted in its challenge of protest against man and of terror before God's wrath (this is only the one side of the Passion and even the Old Testament points beyond it). The covenant of peace stands also above this insurgent and frightful picture of man. God is the One who becomes guilty here and reconciles. And so the limit becomes visible, *total help* over against *total guilt*. This is the last thing, as it is also the first, that God is present and His kindness is still unending. But the significance of this can only become clear in a later context. We must pass on to a consideration, which is interposed in a remarkable fashion, namely, 'under Pontius Pilate'.

16

UNDER PONTIUS PILATE

In virtue of the name of Pontius Pilate being connected with Him, the life and passion of Jesus Christ is an event in the same world-history, in which our life also takes place. And by the co-operation of this politician it acquires outwardly the character of an action in which the divine appointment and righteousness, as well as human perversion and the unrighteousness of the State's ordering of what takes place in the world, become effective and manifest.

HOW does Pontius Pilate come into the Creed? Somewhat coarsely and bitingly, the answer might first of all be: like a dog into a nice room! In the way in which politics get into human life and then in one form or another into the Church also! Who is Pontius Pilate? Really an unpleasant and inconsiderable figure with a very unedifying character. Who is Pontius Pilate? That extremely subordinate functionary, a sort of commandant in the military government of an alien occupying power in Jerusalem. What is he doing there? The local Jewish community has passed a resolution, for the execution of which it had not sufficient authority. It has brought in a death sentence, and must now bring in the legalising and executive power of Pilate. And after some hesitation, he does what is required of him. A very insignificant man in a quite external rôle; for everything important, everything spiritual is played out between Israel and Christ in the Sanhedrin which accuses and rejects Him. Pilate stands by in his uniform and is used, and his rôle is not honourable; he acknowledges that the Man is innocent and yet he hands Him over to death. He was bound to act according to strict law, but does not do so and lets himself be determined by 'political considerations'. He does not venture to stand by the legal decision, but yields to the popular cry and gives Jesus up. He has the Crucifixion carried out by his cohorts. When in the midst of the Confession of the Christian Church, at the moment when we are on the point of stepping into the area of God's deepest mystery, such things come into view, one might well ejaculate with Goethe, 'A foul business! Fie! A political trick!' But there it is, 'under

Pontius Pilate . . .'; and so we must ask ourselves what this means. The novelist, Dorothy L. Sayers, has written a play for the English radio, *The Man born to be King*, and in it interprets the dream of Procla, the wife of Pilate, to the effect that this woman heard in a dream, right through the centuries, as it were, in every language, this thing called out: 'Suffered under Pontius Pilate'. How comes Pontius Pilate into the Creed?

This name in connexion with the Passion of Christ makes it unmistakably clear that this Passion of Jesus Christ, this unveiling of man's rebellion and of God's wrath, yet also of His mercy, did not take place in heaven or in some remote planet or even in some world of ideas; it took place in our time, in the centre of the world-history in which our human life is played out. So we must not escape from this life. We must not take flight to a better land, or to some height or other unknown, nor to any spiritual Cloud-Cuckooland nor to a Christian fairyland. God has come into our life in its utter unloveliness and frightfulness. That the Word became flesh also means that it became temporal, historical. It assumed the form which belongs to the human creature, in which there are such folk as this very Pontius Pilate—the people we belong to and who are also ourselves at any time on a slightly larger scale! It is not necessary to close our eyes to this, for God has not closed His either; He has entered into it all. The Incarnation of the Word is an extremely concrete event, in which a human name may play a part. God's Word has the character of the *hic et nunc*. There is nothing in the opinion of Lessing that God's Word is an 'eternal truth of reason', and not an 'accidental truth of history'. God's history is indeed an accidental truth of history, like this petty commandant. God was not ashamed to exist in this accidental state. To the factors which determined our human time and human history belong, in virtue of the name Pontius Pilate, the life and Passion of Jesus as well. We are not left alone in this frightful world. Into this alien land God has come to us.

To be sure, it is clear that this very fact that Jesus Christ under Pontius Pilate can only suffer and die, characterises this world-history as an extremely questionable one. Here it becomes obvious that we have to do with the passing world, the old era, the world whose typical representative, Pontius Pilate, confronts Jesus in complete powerlessness and helplessness. The Roman world-power is exposed, as Pilate the lieutenant of the great lord in Rome is exposed. This is how the whole political action appears in the light of the approaching Kingdom of God: everything making for a break-up and contradicted in advance. That is the one side: this world into which Christ has come, is illumined by Him in its complete frailty and folly.

But it would not be right to stop here. For the Pilate episode in all four Gospels has still too much importance, for us to be satisfied with stating that Pilate is just the man of this world in general. He is not only that, but he is the statesman and politician; so the meeting here between the world and God's kingdom is indeed a special one. It is not a matter of the meeting between God's Kingdom and human knowledge, human society, human work, but of the meeting between God's Kingdom and the *polis*. Pilate thus stands for the order which confronts the other order represented by Israel and the Church. He is the representative of the Emperor Tiberius. He represents world-history, so far as at all times it is ordered on State lines. That Jesus Christ suffered under Pontius Pilate therefore means also that He did subscribe to this State order. 'Thou hadst had no power over me, except it had been given thee from above.' Jesus Christ is completely serious when He says, 'Give unto Caesar what is Caesar's'. He gives him what is his; He does not attack the authority of Pilate. He suffers, but he does not protest against Pilate having to utter the judgment upon Him. In other words the State order, the *polis*, is the area in which His action too, the action of the eternal Word of God, takes place. It is the area in which, according to human insight, under the threat and application of physical force, the decision is taken as to right and wrong in the external life of men. That is the State, that is what we call politics. Everything that takes place in the realm of politics is somehow an application of this attempt. What takes place in the world is always ordered by the State as well, although fortunately not only by the State! In the midst of this State-ordered world Jesus Christ now appears. By suffering under Pontius Pilate He too participates in this order, and so it is worth while considering what this fact must signify, how the outward order looks, how the whole Pontius Pilate reality looks from the standpoint of the suffering Lord.

This is not the place to evolve the Christian doctrine of the State, which is not to be separated from the Christian doctrine of the Church. Still, a few words should be said here, for in this meeting of Jesus and Pilate everything is together *in nuce* that should be thought and said from the side of the Gospel regarding the realm of the *polis*.

State order, State power, as represented by Pontius Pilate *vis-à-vis* Jesus, is made visible in its negative form, in all its human perversion and unrighteousness. One may indeed say that if anywhere the State is visible as the State of wrong, it is here; and if anywhere the State has been exposed and politics has proved itself to be a monster, then once more it is here. What does Pilate do? He does what politicians have more or less always done and what has always belonged to the actual achievement of politics in all times: he attempts to rescue and maintain order in Jerusalem and thereby at the same time to preserve his own position of power, by surrendering the clear law, for the protection of which he was actually installed. Remarkable contradiction! His duty is to decide upon right and wrong; that is his *raison d'être*; and in order to be able to stay in his position he, 'from fear of the Jews', renounced doing really the very thing he was bound to do: he gives way. True, he does not condemn Jesus—he *cannot* condemn Him, he finds Him not guilty—and yet he surrenders Him. In surrendering Jesus, he is surrendering himself. By becoming the prototype of all persecutors of the Church and by Nero coming to view in him, by the unrighteous State, that is, entering into action there, it is the State as such that is disgraced. In the person of Pilate the State withdraws from the basis of its own existence and becomes a den of robbers, a gangster State, the ordering of an irresponsible clique. *That* is the *polis*, *that* is politics. What wonder that one prefers to cover one's face before it? And if the State has for years and decades long shown itself in this guise only, what wonder that one tires of the whole realm of politics? In fact the State so regarded, the State after the pattern of the Pilates, is the *polis* in its sheer opposition to the Church and to the kingdom of God. This is the State as it is described in the New Testament, in Revelations 13, as the Beast from the abyss, with the other beast of the great muzzle which accompanies it, which the first Beast is continually glorifying and praising. The passion of Christ becomes the unmasking, the judging, the condemnation of this Beast, whose name is *polis*.

But that is not all and we cannot halt there. If Pilate, first of all, brings to view the deterioration of the State and so the unrighteous State, we must also not fail to recognise in this concave mirror the supreme good order of God which is here set up and remains and is effective, the *righteous* State, which is, indeed, disgraced by unrighteous human actions, but can as little as the right Church be completely set aside, because it rests upon divine institution and appointment. The power which Pilate has is no less given him from above because he misuses it. Jesus acknowledged it, exactly in the way in which later on Paul summoned the Roman Christians to acknowledge, even in Nero's state, the divine appointment and institution, to conform to this ordering and thus to renounce all non-political Christianity, and rather to recognise their responsibility for the maintenance of the State. That the order of the State is as such an order of God is indeed also clear in Pilate's case, in that—while as a *bad* statesman he gives Jesus over to death, he still cannot but, as a proper statesman, declare Him to be innocent. And also it becomes visible with uncanny force, that Pilate the bad statesman has power to will and to do the very opposite of what as a proper statesman he ought to have willed and done—to release Barabbas and put Jesus to death, and therefore (so differently from the way it is meant in 1 Peter 2. 14!) 'to reward the wicked, to punish the good'—but that in the result, (which does not excuse him, but which justifies the wisdom of God!) he must also fulfil the supreme law. That Jesus the righteous man should die in place of the unrighteous man, that accordingly this man—Barabbas!—should go free in Jesus' place, was indeed the will of God in the suffering of Jesus Christ. And in this way it is His suffering under Pontius Pilate, the bad statesman—righteous against his will. And that was the will of God in the suffering of Jesus Christ, that Jesus should be delivered by the Jews to the heathen, that the Word of God might come out of the narrow realm of the nation Israel into the Gentile world. The Gentile who accepts Jesus—from the filthy hands of Judas, of the high priests and the people of Jerusalem, he himself a man with filthy hands—this Gentile is the wicked statesman, Pontius Pilate—righteous against his will! He is also in this respect, as Hamann has called him, the executor of the New Testament, in a certain sense practically the founder of the Church of Jews and Gentiles. Thus Jesus triumphs over him, under whose wickedness He has to suffer. Thus Jesus triumphs over the world, in which by treading it He has to suffer. Thus He is the Lord also where He is rejected of men. Thus the political order itself, irrespective of its corruption through human guilt when Jesus was subjected to it, is bound to make it plain that it is in truth subjected to Him. That is why Christians pray for their governors. That is why they make themselves responsible for their maintenance. That is why it is a Christian's task to seek the best for the city, to honour the divine appointment and institution of the State, by choosing and desiring to the best of their knowledge not the wrong, but the right State, the State which makes of the fact that it has its power 'from above', not, like Pilate, a dishonour, but an honour. And beyond that they are confident that God's law in political life, even where it is ignored of men and trodden under foot, is the stronger part, just because of Jesus' Passion—the Jesus to whom *all* power in heaven and on earth is given. Provision is made for bad, petty Pilate to have his trouble for nothing in the long run. How in that case could a Christian take sides with him?

17

WAS CRUCIFIED, DEAD, AND BURIED, HE DESCENDED INTO HELL

In the death of Jesus Christ God has humiliated Himself and rendered Himself up, in order to accomplish His law upon sinful man by taking his place and thus once for all removing from him to Himself the curse that affects him, the punishment he deserves, the past he is hurrying to meet, the abandonment into which he has fallen.

THE mystery of the Incarnation unfolds into the mystery of Good Friday and of Easter. And once more it is as it has been so often in this whole mystery of faith, that we must always see two things together, we must always understand one by the other. In the history of the Christian faith it has, indeed, always been the case that the knowledge of Christians has gravitated more to the one side or to the other. We may take it that the Western Church, the Church of the Occident, has a decided inclination towards the *theologia crucis*—that is, towards bringing out and emphasising the fact that He was surrendered for our transgressions. Whereas the Eastern Church brings more into the foreground the fact that He was raised for our justification, and so inclines towards the *theologia gloriae*. In this matter there is no sense in wanting to play off one against the other. You know that from the beginning Luther strongly worked out the Western tendency—not *theologia gloriae* but *theologia crucis*. What Luther meant by that is right. But we ought not to erect and fix any opposition; for there is no *theologia crucis* which does not have its complement in the *theologia gloriae*. Of course, there is no Easter without Good Friday, but equally certainly there is no Good Friday without Easter! Too much tribulation and sullenness are too easily wrought into Christianity. But if the Cross is the Cross of Jesus Christ and not a speculation on the Cross, which fundamentally any heathen might also have, then it cannot for one second be forgotten or overlooked that the Crucified rose again from the dead the third day. We shall in that case celebrate Good Friday quite differently, and perhaps it would be well not to sing on Good Friday the doleful, sad Passion hymns, but to begin to sing Easter hymns. It is not a sad and miserable business that took place on Good Friday; for He rose again. I wanted to say this first, that you are not to take abstractly what we have to say about the death and the Passion of Christ, but already to look beyond it to the place where His glory is revealed.

This core of Christology has been described in the old theology under two main concepts of the *exinanitio* and the *exaltatio* of Christ. What is the meaning here of humiliation, and of exaltation?

The humiliation of Christ includes the whole, beginning with 'suffered under Pontius Pilate', and decisively visible in 'was crucified, dead, and buried, He descended into hell'. It is certainly first the humiliation of this man who suffers there and dies and passes into the outmost darkness. But what first gives its significance to the humiliation and abandonment of this man is the fact that this man is God's Son, and it is none other than God Himself who humbles and surrenders Himself in Him.

And so when this is countered by the exaltation of Jesus Christ as the mystery of Easter, this glorifying is certainly a self-glorifying of God; it is His honour that triumphs there: 'God goes up with a shout'. But the real mystery of Easter is not that God is glorified in it, but that man is exalted, raised to the right hand of God and permitted to triumph over sin, death and the devil.

When we hold these two things together, then the picture before us is that of an inconceivable exchange, of a *katalage*, that is, a substitution. Man's reconciliation with God takes place through God's putting Himself in man's place and man's being put in God's place, as a sheer act of grace. It is this inconceivable miracle which is our reconciliation.

When the Confession itself already stresses this 'crucified, dead and buried . . .' in a purely external way by the explicitness and completeness of an enumeration which is not superabundant in words; moreover, when the Gospels draw out the Crucifixion story to such an extent, and when at all times the Cross of Jesus repeatedly comes to the fore as the real centre of the entire Christian faith; when in all centuries there was heard again and again, *Ave crux unica spe mea*, we have to be clear that the point is not the glorification and emphasis of the martyr death of a

religious founder—there are doubtless tales of martyrs which
are more impressive, but with that we are not concerned—yet
neither is it the expression of universal world-sorrow over the
Cross as a kind of symbol of the limit of human existence. Thereby
we remove ourselves from the knowledge of those who have
attested the crucified Jesus Christ. In the sense of the Apostolic
witness the Crucifixion of Jesus Christ is the concrete deed and
action of God Himself. God changes Himself, God Himself comes
most near, God thinks it not robbery to be divine, that is, He does
not hold on to the booty like a robber, but God parts with Himself. Such is the glory of His Godhead, that He can be 'selfless',
that He can actually forgive Himself something. He remains
genuinely true to Himself, but just through not having to limit
Himself to His Godhead. It is the depth of the Godhead, the
greatness of His glory which is revealed in the very fact that
it can also completely hide itself in its sheer opposite, in the profoundest rejection and the greatest misery of the creature. What
takes place in the Crucifixion of Christ is that God's Son takes to
Himself that which must come to the creature existing in revolt,
which wants to deliver itself from its creatureliness and itself be
the Creator. He puts Himself into this creature's need and does
not abandon it to itself. Moreover, He does not only help it from
without and greet it only from afar off; He makes the misery of
His creature His own. To what end? So that His creature may go
out freely, so that the burden which it has laid upon itself may be
borne, borne away. The creature itself must have gone to pieces,
but God does not want that; He wants it to be saved. So great is
the ruin of the creature that less than the self-surrender of God
would not suffice for its rescue. But so great is God, that it is His
will to render up Himself. Reconciliation means God taking man's
place. Let me add that no doctrine of this central mystery can
exhaustively and precisely grasp and express the extent to which
God has intervened for us here. Do not confuse my theory of the
reconciliation with the thing itself. All theories of reconciliation
can be but pointers. But do also pay attention to this 'for us':
nothing must be deducted from it! Whatever a doctrine of
reconciliation tries to express, it *must* say this.

In the death of Jesus Christ God has accomplished His law.
In the death of Jesus Christ He has acted as Judge towards Man.
Man has betaken himself to the point at which a verdict of God
is pronounced upon him and has inevitably to be carried out.

Man stands before God as a sinner, as a being who has sundered himself from God, who has rebelled against being what he may be. He rebels against grace; it is too little for him, he turns away from gratitude. Such is human life, this constant turning away, this coarse and subtle sinning. This sinning leads man into inconceivable need: he makes himself impossible before God. He puts himself where God cannot see him. He puts himself so to speak behind the back of God's grace. But the back of God's 'Yes' is the divine 'No': it is the judgment. As God's grace is irresistible, so His judgment is irresistible.

And now we have to understand what was declared of Christ, that He was 'crucified, dead and buried . . .', as the expression of that which is now actually accomplished upon man.

Crucified. When an Israelite was crucified, that meant that he was accursed, expelled, not only from the realm of the living but from the covenant with God, removed from the circle of the elect. Crucified means rejected, handed over to the death of the gallows inflicted on the heathen. Let us be clear what is involved in the judgment of God, in what the human creature has to suffer from God's side as a sinful creature; he is involved in rejection, in the curse. 'Cursed is he that dies on the cross.' What befalls Christ is what ought to befall us.

Dead. Death is the end of all present possibilities of life. Dying means exhausting the last of the possibilities given to us. However we wish to interpret dying physically and metaphysically, whatever may happen then, one thing is certain, that then there happens the last action that can happen in creaturely existence. Whatever may happen beyond death must at least be something different from the continuation of this life. Death really means the *end*. That is the judgment under which our life stands: it is waiting for death. To be born and grow up, to ripen and grow old, is to go towards the moment at which for each of us it will be the end, definitely the end. The matter looked at from this side is a matter which makes death into an element in our life, about which we prefer not to think.

Buried. It stands there so unobtrusively and simply superfluously. But it is not there for nothing. Some day we shall be buried. Some day a company of men will proceed out to a churchyard and lower a coffin and everyone will go home; but one will not come back, and that will be me. The seal of death will be that they will bury me as a thing that is superfluous and disturbing in the land of the living. 'Buried' gives to death the character of passing away and decay and to human existence the character of transitoriness and corruptibility. What then is the meaning of man's life? It means hurrying to the grave. Man is hurrying to meet his past. This past, in which there is no more future, will be the final thing: all that we are will have been and will have been corrupted. Perhaps a memory will remain, so long as there are men who like to remember us. But some day they too will die and then this memory too will pass away. There is no great name in human history which will not some day or other have become a forgotten name. That is the meaning of being 'buried'; and that is the judgment on man, that in the grave he drops into forgottenness. That is God's answer to sin: there is nothing else to be done with sinful man, except to bury him and forget him.

Descended into hell. In the Old and New Testaments the picture of hell is somewhat different from what developed out of it later on. Hell, the place of the *inferi*, Hades in the Old Testament sense, is certainly the place of torment, the place of complete separateness, where man continues to exist only as a non-being, as a shadow. The Israelites thought of this place as a place where men continue to hover around like flitting shadows. And the bad thing about this being in hell in the Old Testament sense is that the dead can no longer praise God, they can no longer see His face, they can no longer take part in the Sabbath services of Israel. It is a state of exclusion from God, and that makes death so fearful, makes hell what it is. That man is separated from God means being in the place of torment. 'Wailing and gnashing of teeth'—our imagination is not adequate to this reality, this existence without God. The atheist is not aware of what Godlessness is. Godlessness is existence in hell. What else but this is left as the result of sin? Has not man separated himself from God by his own act? 'Descended into hell' is merely confirmation of it. God's judgment is righteous—that is, it gives man what he wanted. God would not be God, the Creator would not be the Creator, the creature would not be the creature, and man would not be man, if this verdict and its execution could be stayed.

But now the Confession tells us that the execution of this verdict is carried out by God in this way, that He, God Himself, in Jesus Christ His Son, at once true God and true man, takes the place of condemned man. God's judgment is executed, God's law takes its course, but in such a way that what man had to suffer is suffered by this One, who as God's Son stands for all others. Such is the lordship of Jesus Christ, who stands for us before God, by taking upon Himself what belongs to us. In Him God makes Himself liable, at the point at which we are accursed and guilty and lost. He it is in His Son, who in the person of this crucified man bears on Golgotha all that ought to be laid on us. And in this way He makes an end of the curse. It is not God's will that man should perish; it is not God's will that man should pay what he was bound to pay; in other words, God extirpates the sin. And God does this, not in spite of His righteousness, but it is God's very righteousness that He, the holy One, steps in for us the unholy, that He wills to save and does save us. Righteousness in the Old Testament sense is not the righteousness of the judge who makes the debtor pay, but the action of a judge who in the accused recognises the wretch whom he wishes to help by putting him to rights. That is what righteousness means. Righteousness means setting right. And that is what God does. Of course not without the punishment being borne and the whole distress breaking out, but through His putting Himself in the place of the guilty one. He who may and can do this is justified in the fact that He takes over the rôle of His creature. God's mercy and God's righteousness are not at variance with each other.

> 'His Son is not too dear to Him,
> He gives Him up; for He
> From fire eternal by His blood
> Would rescue me.'

That is the mystery of Good Friday.

But actually we are looking away beyond Good Friday, when we say that God comes in our place and takes our punishment upon Himself. Thereby He actually takes it away from us. All pain, all temptation, as well as our dying, is just the shadow of the judgment which God has already executed in our favour. That which in truth was bound to affect us and ought to have affected us, has actually been turned aside from us already in Christ's death. That is attested by Christ's saying on the Cross, 'It is finished!' So then in view of Christ's Cross we are invited on the one hand to realise the magnitude and weight of our sin in what our forgiveness cost. In the strict sense there is no knowledge of sin except in the light of Christ's Cross. For he alone understands what sin is, who knows that his sin is forgiven him. And on the other hand we may realise that the price is paid on our behalf, so that we are acquitted of sin and its consequences. We are no longer addressed and regarded by God as sinners, who must pass under judgment for their guilt. We have nothing more to pay. We are acquitted gratis, *sola gratia*, by God's own entering in for us.

18

THE THIRD DAY HE ROSE AGAIN FROM THE DEAD

In the Resurrection of Jesus Christ man is once for all exalted, and appointed to discover with God his right against all his foes and thus set free to live a new life, in which he no longer has sin and therefore the curse too, death, the grave and hell, in front of him but behind him.

'THE third day He rose again from the dead' is the Easter message. It asserts that not in vain did God humble Himself in His Son; by so doing He assuredly acted also for His own honour and for the confirmation of His glory. By His mercy triumphing in His very humiliation, the result is the exaltation of Jesus Christ. And when we said earlier that in the humiliation God's Son was involved and therefore God Himself, we must now emphasise that what is involved in the exaltation is man. In Jesus Christ man is exalted and appointed to the life for which God has set him free in the death of Jesus Christ. God has so to speak abandoned the sphere of His glory and man may now take this place. That is the Easter message, the goal of reconciliation, man's redemption. It is the goal which was already visible on Good Friday. By God interceding for man—the New Testament writers were not afraid to use the expression 'paying'—man is a ransomed creature. Ἀπολύτρωσις is a legal concept which described the ransoming of a slave. The goal is that man is transferred to another status in law. He no longer belongs to that which had a right over him, to that realm of curse, death and hell; he is translated into the kingdom of God's dear Son. That means that his position, his condition, his legal status as a sinner is rejected in every form. Man is no longer seriously regarded by God as a sinner. Whatever he may be, whatever there is to be said of him, whatever he has to reproach himself with, God no longer takes him seriously as a sinner. He has died to sin; there on the Cross of Golgotha. He is no longer present for sin. He is acknowledged before God and established as a righteous man, as one who does right before God. As he now stands, he has, of course, his existence in sin and so in its guilt; but he has that behind him. The turn has been achieved, once for all. But we cannot say, 'I have turned away once for all, I have experienced'—no; 'once for all' is Jesus Christ's 'once for all'. But if we believe in Him, then it holds for us. Man is in Christ Jesus, who has died for him, in virtue of His Resurrection, God's dear child, who may live by and for the good pleasure of God.

If that is the message of Easter, then you realise that in the Resurrection of Jesus Christ there is the revelation of the still hidden fruit of Christ's death. It is this very turning-point which is still hidden in the death of Christ, hidden under the aspect in which man there appears consumed by the wrath of God. And now the New Testament bears us witness, that this aspect of man is not the meaning of the event upon Golgotha, but that behind this aspect the real meaning of this event is the one which is revealed on the third day. On this third day there begins a new story of man, so that we may even divide the life of Jesus into two great periods, the thirty-three years to His death, and the quite short and decisive period of the forty days between His death and the Ascension. The third day a new life of Jesus begins; but at the same time on the third day there begins a new *Aeon*, a new shape of the world, after the old world has been completely done away and settled in the death of Jesus Christ. Easter is the breaking in of a new time and world in the existence of the man Jesus, who now begins a new life as the conqueror, as the victorious bearer, as the destroyer of the burden of man's sin, which had been laid upon Him. In this altered existence of His the first community saw not only a supernatural continuation of His previous life, but an entirely new life, that of the exalted Jesus Christ, and simultaneously the beginning of a new *world*. (The efforts to relate Easter to certain renewals, such as occur in creaturely life, say in spring or even in man's awakening in the morning, and so on, are without any strength. Upon spring there inexorably follows a winter and upon the awakening a falling asleep. We have to do here with a cyclic movement of becoming new and old. But the becoming new at Easter is a becoming new once for all.) In the resurrection of Jesus Christ the claim is made, according to the New Testament, that God's victory in man's favour in the person of His Son has already been won. Easter is indeed the great pledge of our hope, but simultaneously this future is already present in the Easter message. It is the proclamation of a victory already won. The war is at an end—even though here and there troops are still shooting, because they have not heard anything yet about the capitulation. The game is won, even though the player can still play a few further moves. Actually he is already mated. The clock has run down, even though the pendulum still swings a few times this way and that. It is in this interim space that we are living: the old is past, behold it has all become new. The Easter message tells us that our enemies, sin, the curse and death, are beaten. Ultimately they can no longer start mischief. They still behave as though the game were not decided, the battle not fought; we must still reckon with them, but fundamentally we must cease to fear them any more. If you have heard the Easter message, you can no longer run around with a tragic face and lead the humourless existence of a man who has no hope. One thing still holds, and only this one thing is really serious, that Jesus is the Victor. A seriousness that would look back past this, like Lot's wife, is not *Christian* seriousness. It may be burning behind— and truly it is burning—but we have to look, not at it, but at the other fact, that we are invited and summoned to take seriously the victory of God's glory in this man Jesus and to be joyful in Him. Then we may live in thankfulness and not in fear.

The Resurrection of Jesus Christ reveals, it completes this proclamation of victory. We must not transmute the Resurrection into a spiritual event. We must listen to it and let it tell us the story how there was an empty grave, that new life beyond death did become visible. 'This [man snatched from death] is My beloved Son, in whom I am well pleased.' What was announced at the Baptism in Jordan now becomes an event and manifest. To those who know this, the break between the old world and the new is proclaimed. They have still a tiny stretch to run, till it becomes visible that God in Jesus Christ *has* accomplished all for them.

19

HE ASCENDED INTO HEAVEN, AND SITTETH ON THE RIGHT HAND OF GOD THE FATHER ALMIGHTY

The aim of the work of Jesus Christ, which happened once for all, is the foundation of His Church through the knowledge, entrusted to the witnesses of His resurrection, that the omnipotence of God and the grace of God that are active and apparent in Him are one and the same thing. And so the end of this work is also the beginning of the end-time, that is, of the time in which the Church has to proclaim to all the world the gracious omnipotence and the omnipotent grace of God in Jesus.

THE course of the text of the Confession of Faith shows us outwardly that we are approaching a *goal*, the goal of Jesus Christ's work, so far as it has happened once for all. Of this road there is still a part outstanding, which is future and which will become visible at the close of the Confession, 'from thence He shall come' again. . . . But what has occurred once for all, now stands rounded off before us in a whole series of perfects: begotten, conceived, born, suffered, crucified, dead, buried, descended, rose again; and now suddenly a present: 'He *sitteth* on the right hand of God. . . .' It is as if we had made the ascent of a mountain and had now reached the summit. This present is completed by a final perfect, that He ascended into heaven; which for its part completes the 'rose again from the dead'.

With this 'he sitteth on the right hand of God the Father' we obviously pass into a *new* time which is our present time, the time of the Church, the end-time, inaugurated and founded by the work of Jesus Christ. In the New Testament the report of this event constitutes the conclusion of the reports of Jesus Christ's Resurrection. There is—almost analogous to the Christmas miracle—a relatively thin line in the New Testament, which speaks of Christ's ascent into heaven. Here and there only the Resurrection is mentioned and then directly the session on the right hand of the Father. In the Gospel too the ascent to heaven is relatively sparingly mentioned. What is involved is this transition, the change from revelation time to our time.

What is the meaning of the Ascension? According to what we have said about heaven and earth, it means at any rate that Jesus leaves earthly space, the space, that is, which is conceivable to us and which He has sought out for our sakes. He no longer belongs to it as we belong to it. That does not mean that it becomes alien to Him, that this space is not His space too. On the contrary, since He stands *above* this space, He fulfils it and He becomes present to it. But now, of course, no longer in the way at the time of His revelation and of His earthly activity. The Ascension does not mean that Christ has passed over into that other realm of the creaturely world, into the realm of what is inconceivable to us. 'On the right hand of God' means not only the transition from the conceivable to the inconceivable in the created world. Jesus is removed in the direction of the mystery of *divine* space, which is utterly concealed from man. It is not heaven that is His abode; He is with God. The Crucified and Risen One is where God is. The goal of His activity on earth and in history is that He goes thither. Involved in the Incarnation and in the Crucifixion is the humiliation of God. But in the Resurrection of Jesus Christ is involved the exaltation of man. Christ is now, as the Bearer of humanity, as our Representative, in the place where God is and in the way in which God is. Our flesh, our human nature, is exalted in Him to God. The end of His work is that we are with Him above. We with Him beside God.

From this starting point we have to look backwards and forwards. If we understand the New Testament correctly, with its witness to this outcome of the life and activity of Jesus Christ, this outcome is characterised in a twofold way.

1. From this Last One there rises a light, which is seen by His Apostles. Conclusive knowledge is entrusted to the witnesses of His Resurrection. In the Gospel according to St. Matthew there stand the words of Christ (28. 18): 'All power is given unto me in heaven and in earth.' It is sensible and necessary to bring these words into connexion with the session at the right hand of God the Father Almighty. The concept of omnipotence appears at both points. In Ephesians 4. 10 the same knowledge is expressed: 'He hath ascended up heavenwards, that He might fill all things . . .'; fill them with His will and His word. He is now in the highest;

He is now the Lord and revealed as such. We come back at this passage to things which we touched upon in the exposition of the first article. If we speak correctly of God the Almighty who is over all things, then we must never understand by God's omnipotence anything else than the reality of which the second article speaks. The knowledge which the Apostles acquired on the basis of Christ's Resurrection, the conclusion of which is the Ascension of Christ, is essentially this basic knowledge that the reconciliation which took place in Jesus Christ is not some casual story, but that in this work of God's grace we have to do with the word of *God's omnipotence*, that here an ultimate and supreme thing comes into action, behind which there is no other reality. There is no getting beyond this event, of which the second and third articles speak. Christ is He who has *all* powers, and with Him we have to do, if we believe. And conversely, God's omnipotence is revealed and active entirely in the grace of the reconciliation of Jesus Christ. The grace of God and the omnipotence of God are identical. We must never understand the one without the other. Here again we have to do with the revelation of the mystery of the Incarnation, that this man is God's Son and God's Son is this man. Jesus Christ has this place, this function over against us and He has them in ultimate reality. He stands in relation to God as the One to whom the power of God is absolutely entrusted; like a Governor or a Prime Minister, to whom His King has transferred His whole power. Jesus Christ speaks as God and acts as God; and conversely, if we would know God's speech and action, we need look only upon this man. This identity of God and man in Jesus Christ is the knowledge, the revelation of the knowledge, by which the work of Jesus Christ, accomplished once for all, has reached its conclusion.

2. 'He sitteth on the right hand of God the Father'—the summit has been reached, the perfect tenses lie behind us and we enter the realm of the present. That is what we have to say of our time—that is the first and the last thing that matters for our existence in time. At its basis lies this existence of Jesus Christ, His sitting at the right hand of God the Father. Whatever prosperity or defeat may occur in our space, whatever may become and pass away, there is one constant, one thing that remains and continues, this sitting of His at the right hand of God the Father. There is no historical turning-point which approaches this. Here we have the mystery of what we term world history, Church

history, history of civilisation; here we have the thing that under-
lies everything. This first of all quite simply means the thing that
is expressed again at the end of St. Matthew's Gospel by the so-
called missionary mandate: 'Go ye into all the world and make
disciples of all the nations, baptising them and teaching them to
observe all things whatsoever I command you.' Consequently
that knowledge, that 'God's omnipotence is God's grace', is no
idle knowledge. And the conclusion of revelation time is not the
end of a spectacle, where the curtain falls and the onlookers may
go home, but it ends with a challenge, with a command. The
salvation event now becomes a bit of world event. What now
becomes visible to the Apostles corresponds to the fact that here
too on earth, as a human history, as an action of the disciples,
there is an earthly place corresponding to the heavenly place, a
life and action of the witnesses of His Resurrection. With the
departure of Jesus Christ to the Father an establishment on earth
is made. His departure means not only an end but also a beginning, even though not as the continuation of His advent. For it
should not be said that the work of Jesus Christ simply continues
in the life of Christians and the existence of the Church. The life
of the saints is not a prolongation of the revelation of Jesus Christ
upon earth. That would contradict His 'It is finished'. What
happened in Jesus Christ needs no continuation. But, of course,
what happened once for all possesses in what now happens upon
earth a correspondence, a reflection; not a repetition but a likeness. And all that Christian life is in faith in Christ, all that is
called the community, is this likeness, this shadowing forth of the
existence of Jesus Christ as the Head of His body. Christ founds
His Church by going to the Father, by making Himself known
to His Apostles. This knowledge means the call to 'Go into all
the world and proclaim the Gospel to every creature'. Christ
is the Lord. That is what all creation, what all nations should
know. The conclusion of Christ's work is therefore not an opportunity given to the Apostles for idleness, but it is their being sent
out into the world. Here there is no rest possible; here there is
rather a running and racing; here is the start of the mission, the
sending of the Church into the world and for the world.

This time which now breaks in, the time of the Church, is at
the same time the end-time, the final time, the time in which the
existence or the meaning of the existence of the creaturely world
reaches its goal. We heard, when we spoke of Christ's Cross and

Resurrection, that the battle was won, the clock had run down, but still God has patience, God is still waiting. For this time of His patience He has put the Church into the world, and the meaning of this last time is, that it is filled up by the message of the Gospel and that the world has this command, to listen to this message. We may name this time which broke in with Jesus Christ's Ascension into heaven, 'the time of the Word', perhaps also the time of the abandonment and, in a certain respect, of the loneliness of the Church on earth. It is the time in which the Church is united with Christ only in faith and by the Holy Spirit; it is the interim time between His earthly existence and His return in glory; it is the time of the great opportunity, of the task of the Church towards the world; it is the time of mission. As we said, it is the time of God's patience, in which He is waiting for the Church, and, with the Church, for the world. For what has occurred conclusively in Jesus Christ as the fullness of the time, is obviously not to be accomplished apart from man's participation, apart from the praise to God from their lips, apart from their ears, which ought to hear the Word, apart from their feet and hands, by which they ought to become messengers of the Gospel. That God and man have become one in Jesus Christ should be visible first in the fact that there are men of God on earth, who are permitted to be His witnesses. Church time, end-time, final time—what makes time so significant and great, is not that it is final time, but that it leaves room for hearing, believing and repenting, for proclaiming and comprehending the message. It is the time which stands to Jesus Christ in the relationship of 'Behold I stand at the door and knock'. He is most near. He wishes to enter; already quite near and yet outside, still before the door, and already we within may hear Him and be expectant of His entry.—Into this interim time and end-time, into this time of waiting and of the divine patience there now comes that twofold order of the divine providence, the connexions between Church and State, of the inward and the outward spheres in their opposition and their co-ordination. They are not the last order or the last word; but, correctly understood, they are the good ordering to the goal, which corresponds with the grace of God. The Ascension is the beginning of this time of ours.

20

THE COMING OF JESUS CHRIST THE JUDGE

The Church's recollection is also its expectation, and its message to the world is also the world's hope. For Jesus Christ, from whose word and work the Church knowingly, the world as yet unknowingly, derives, is the same who comes to meet the Church and the world, as the goal of the time that is coming to an end, in order to make visible, finally and for all people, the decision taken in Him—God's grace and kingdom as the measure by which the whole of humanity and every single human existence is measured.

'. . . FROM thence He shall come to judge the quick and the dead.' After many perfects and the present there now follows the future—'He shall come'. We might parse the whole of the second article in three tenses, that He *came*, that He *sitteth* on the right hand of God, and that He *shall come again*.

First let me say something about the Christian concept of time. We cannot but realise that here a quite strange light falls upon what in the genuine and proper sense is called real time—time in the light of God's time, eternity.

Jesus Christ's having come, all those past tenses, would answer to what we term the past. But how inappropriate it would be to say of that event that it was past. What Jesus suffered and did is certainly not past; it is rather the old that is past, the world of man, the world of disobedience and disorder, the world of misery, sin and death. Sin has been cancelled, death has been vanquished. Sin and death *did exist*, and the whole of world history, including that which ran its course *post Christum*, right down to our day, *existed*. All that is past in Christ; we can only think back on all that.

But Jesus Christ sitteth beside the Father, as He who has suffered and has risen from the dead. That is the present. Since He is present as God is present, it already admits of being said that He shall come again as the person He once was. He who is to-day just as He was yesterday, will also be the same to-morrow—

Jesus Christ yesterday and to-day and the same to eternity. Since Jesus Christ exists as the person He was, obviously He is the beginning of a new, different time from that which we know, a time in which there is no fading away, but real time which has a yesterday, a to-day and a to-morrow. But Jesus Christ's yester-day is also His to-day and His to-morrow. It is not timelessness, not empty eternity that comes in place of His time. His time is not at an end; it continues in the movement from yesterday to to-day, into to-morrow. It has not the frightful fleetingness of our present. When Jesus Christ sitteth at the right hand of the Father, this existence of His with God, His existence as the possessor and representative of the divine grace and power towards us men, has nothing to do with what we are foolishly wont to conceive as eternity—namely, an existence without time. If this existence of Jesus Christ at the right hand of God is real existence and as such the measure of all existence, then it is also existence in time, although in another time than the one we know. If the lordship and rule of Jesus Christ at the Father's right hand is the meaning of what we see as the existence of our world history and our life-history, then this existence of Jesus Christ is not a timeless existence, and eternity is not a timeless eternity. Death is timeless, nothingness is timeless. So we men are timeless when we are without God and without Christ. Then we have no time. But this timelessness He has overcome. Christ has time, the fullness of time. He sitteth at the right hand of God as He who has come, who has acted and suffered and triumphed in death. His session at God's right hand is not just the extract of this history; it is the eternal within this history.

And corresponding to this eternal existence of Christ there is also His becoming existent. What was, comes; what happened will happen. He is the Alpha and the Omega, the centre of real time, of God's time; which is not meaningless time that passes away. Not the present as we know it, in which every 'now' is just the leap from a no-longer into a not-yet. Is that the present, this fluttering in the shadow of Hades? In the life of Jesus Christ another present meets us, which is its own past, and so not a timelessness which leads into nothingness. And when it says that Christ is coming again, this coming again is not a goal lying in the infinite. 'Infiniteness' is a comfortless business and not a divine predicate, but one that pertains to fallen creatureliness. This end without an end is frightful. It is an image of man's lostness. Man is in such a state that he is precipitated into aim-lessness and endlessness. This ideal of the endless has nothing to do at all with God. A limit is rather set to this time. Jesus Christ is and brings the real time. But God's time also has an end, as well as a beginning and a middle. Man is surrounded and upheld on all sides. That is life. So man's existence becomes visible in the second article: Jesus Christ with His past, present and future.

When the Christian community looks back at what happened in Christ, at His first Advent, His life, death and Resurrection, when it lives in this recollection, then it is not mere recollection, not what we call history. That which has happened once for all has rather the power of divine *presence*. What happened still happens, and as such will happen. The point from which the Christian community derives, with its confession of Jesus Christ, is the same point as that which it goes to meet. Its recollection is also its expectation. And when the Christian community ap-proaches the world, then its message at first glance has certainly the character of an historical narrative, then the talk is of Jesus of Nazareth, who suffered under Pontius Pilate, after having been born under the Emperor Augustus. But woe if the Christian message to the world were to halt at this event. The content and object of this narrative would then inevitably be a man who lived once upon a time, or a legendary figure to which many nations look back in a similar fashion, one founder of a religion among others. How deceived then the world would be about what did and does exist in truth, about the good news that 'Christ hath appeared, for us to atone; rejoice, O Christendom!' This perfect 'Christ hath appeared' must also be proclaimed in its actuality over against the world as the thing which the world too may hope, which world history too is going to meet.

And again, Christian faith could be regarded as expectation and hope; but this expectation could be of an empty and general character. One hopes for better times, better circumstances on 'this side', or in the form of another life in the so-called 'beyond'. Thus lightly the Christian hope melts into an indeterminate expectation of some sort of dreamed-of glory. One forgets the real content and object of the Christian expectation—namely, that He who comes is He who was. We are going to meet Him from whom we come. That must also, in the relation between the Church and the world, be the substance of its message: it does not point into the void when it gives courage and hope for men; it may give courage and hope in view of what has happened. 'It is finished' is completely valid. The Christian perfect is not an imperfect; but the rightly understood perfect has the force of the future. 'My times are in Thy hand!' So we wander like Elijah in the strength of this food forty days and forty nights to the Mount of God, which is called Horeb. It is still wandering and it is still not the goal, but wandering directed by the goal. That is how we Christians ought to speak to the non-Christians. We must not sit among them like melancholy owls, but in a certainty about our goal, which surpasses all other certainty. Yet how often we stand ashamed beside the children of the world, and how we must understand them if our message will not satisfy them. He who knows that 'our times are in Thy hand' will not haughtily regard the men of the world, who, in a definite hope that often ashames us, go their way; but he will understand them better than they understand themselves. He will see their hope as a parable, a sign that the world is not abandoned, but has a beginning and a goal. We Christians have to put the right Alpha and Omega into the heart of this secular thought and hope. But we can only do so if we surpass the world in confidence.

So the situation is, that the world derives unknowingly, while the Church derives knowingly from Jesus Christ, from His work. The objective fact is that Jesus Christ has come and that He has spoken His word and done His work. That *exists*, quite independently of whether we men believe it or not. This holds for *all*, for the Christians and for the non-Christians. We derive from the fact that Christ has come and we ought to regard the world accordingly. That the world is 'worldly' goes without saying. But it is the world in the midst of which Jesus Christ was crucified and rose again. The Church also comes from there and is in the same position as the world. But the Church is the place where one knows that, and that is indeed a tremendous difference between the Church and the world. We Christians may know it, we may see with open eyes the light which has arisen, the light of the parousia. Therein lies a special grace, about which we may be glad every morning. We really have not deserved this grace; the Christians are no better than the children of the world. Therefore it can only be a matter of their showing, out of their knowledge, something to the others who do not know. They must let the tiny light shine, which has been given to them.

And the Church and the world both have before them Him

from whom they derive. And for both the miracle is that this goal of hope does not stand somewhere and we must laboriously build the road to it, but that it says in the Confession *Venturus est.* Not that we must come; it is He who comes. Where would we arrive, with our wandering and running? World history with its industry, with its wars and its armistices, the history of civilisation with its illusions and improbabilities—is that a way? We have to smile. But when He comes, He who is the Actor, then from there all that is so miserable in our 'progressiveness' is drawn into a different light. The frightful folly and weakness of the Church and of the world are lit up by Him. 'Christ is born.' Once again it is Advent. Christ's coming again is the coming of Him who was there. Thereby the folly of the heathen and the weakness of the Church are not excused, but they enter the light of Easter Day: 'The world was lost, Christ was born'. Yet Christ not only did intercede for us; He will also intercede for us. In this way human and Christian existence is maintained both from its start and from its finish. Christ has not been and will not be ashamed of being called our Brother.

'. . . From thence He shall come.' In this 'from thence' is contained above all this fact, that He will issue out of the hiddenness in which He still remains for us to-day, where He is proclaimed and believed by the Church, where He is present to us only in His Word. The New Testament says of this future coming that 'He shall come on the clouds of heaven with great power and glory' and 'as the lightning goeth out from East to West, so shall be the coming of the Son of man'. These are metaphors, but metaphors of ultimate realities, which at least indicate that it takes place no longer in secrecy but is completely revealed. No one will any more be able to deceive himself about this being reality. So He will come. He will rend the heavens and stand before us as the person He is, sitting at the right hand of the Father. He comes in the possession and in the exercise of the divine omnipotence. He comes as the One in whose hands our entire existence is enclosed. Him we are expecting, He is coming and He will be manifest as the One whom we know already. It has all taken place; the only thing wanting is that the covering be removed and all may see it. He has already accomplished it and He has power to make it manifest. In His hand stands the real time and not that endless time in which we never have time. Even now this fullness may exist. Our life has a fulfilment and that fulfilment will be made manifest. Our future consists in our being shown that all was right and good in our existence and in this evil world-history and—miracle on miracle!—in the still more evil Church history. We do not see it: what is in Heussi is not good, and what is in the newspapers is not good. And yet some day it will be manifest that it was right, because Christ was in the centre. He rules, seated at the Father's right hand. That will come to light and all tears will be wiped away. That is the miracle which we may go to meet and which in Jesus Christ will be shown to us as that which already exists, when He shall come in His glory, like a lightning flash which lightens from the East even unto the West.

'. . . To judge the quick and the dead.' If we wish to understand aright here, we must from the start repress certain pictures of the world-judgment, as far as we can, and make an effort not to think of what they are describing. All those visions, as the great painters represent them, about the judging of the world (Michael Angelo in the Sistine Chapel), Christ advancing with clenched fist and dividing those on the right from those on the left, while one's glance remains fixed on those on the left! The painters have imagined to some extent with delight how these damned folk sink in the pool of hell. But that is certainly not the point. Question 52 of the Heidelberg Catechism asks: 'What comfort hast thou by the coming again of Christ to judge the quick and the dead?' Answer: 'That in all my miseries and persecutions I look with my head erect for the very same, who before yielded Himself unto the judgment of God for me and took away all malediction from me, to come Judge from heaven. . . .' A different note is struck here. Jesus Christ's return to judge the quick and the dead is tidings of joy. 'With head erect', the Christian, the Church may and ought to confront this future. For He that comes is the same who previously offered Himself to the judgment of God. It is His return we are looking for. Would it had been vouchsafed to Michael Angelo and the other artists to hear and see this!

Jesus Christ's coming again for judgment, His ultimate and universal manifestation is often described in the New Testament as *the* revelation. He will be revealed, not only to the Church but to everyone, as the Person He is. He will not only then be the judge, He is that already; but then for the first time it will become visible, that it is not a question of our Yes and No, our faith or lack of faith. In full clarity and publicity the 'it is finished' will

come to light. For that the Church is waiting; and without knowing it the world is waiting too. We are all on the way to meet this
manifestation of that which is. It does not seem as yet that
God's grace and justice are really valid as the measure by which
the whole of humanity and each individual is measured. Still we
have doubts and anxieties as to whether they really hold. There
is still room for righteousness by works and boasting by the pious
as well as by the godless. It can still seem that this is not so. The
Church proclaims Christ and the decision made in Him. But it too
still lives in this time that is drawing to a close and carries all the
marks of great weakness in itself. What is the future bringing?
Not, once more, a turning-point in history, but the revelation of
that which is. It is the future, but the future of that which the
Church remembers, of that which has already taken place once
and for all. The Alpha and the Omega are the same thing. The
return of Jesus Christ will prove Goethe to be right, that

> '*God's is the East and God's the West;*
> *In North and South do rest the lands*
> *Deep in the peace of God's own hands.*'

In the Biblical world of thought the judge is not primarily the
one who rewards some and punishes the others; he is the man who
creates order and restores what has been destroyed. We may go to
meet this judge, this restoration or, better, the revelation of this
restoration with unconditioned confidence, because *He* is the
judge. With unconditioned confidence, because we come from
His revelation. The present time seems so petty and wretched and
will not satisfy us, not even the present time of the Church and
Christendom! But it is Christendom which may and ought to
let itself be called again and again, called back to its origin and
at the same time to meet the future of Jesus Christ, the gleaming
and glorious future of God Himself, who is the same yesterday and to-day and therefore to-morrow as well. To the seriousness of the thought of judgment no injury will be done, for there
it will be manifest that God's grace and God's right are the
measure by which the whole of humanity and each man will be
measured. *Venturus judicare*: God knows everything that exists
and happens. Then we may well be terrified, and to that extent
those visions of the Last Judgment are not simply meaningless.
That which is not of God's grace and right cannot exist. Infinitely
much human as well as Christian 'greatness' perhaps plunges

there into the outermost darkness. That there is such a divine No is indeed included in this *judicare*. But the moment we grant this we must revert to the truth that the Judge who puts some on the left and the others on the right, is in fact He who has yielded Himself to the judgment of God *for me* and has taken away all malediction from me. It is He who died on the Cross and rose at Easter. The fear of God in Jesus Christ can be none other than that which stands in the joy and confidence of the question: 'In what doth Christ's coming again comfort thee?' That does not lead to Apokatastasis. There is a decision and a division, but by Him who has interceded for us. Is there even to-day a sharper division and a more urgent challenge than the message about this Judge?

21

I BELIEVE IN THE HOLY GHOST

When men belong to Jesus Christ in such a way that they have
freedom to recognise His word as addressed also to them, His work
as done also for them, the message about Him as also their task;
and then for their part, freedom to hope for the best for all other
men, this happens, indeed, as their human experience and action,
and yet not in virtue of their human capacity, determination and
exertion, but solely on the basis of the free gift of God, in which all
this is given to them. In this giving and gift God is the Holy
Spirit.

AT this point the Creed once more repeats the words 'I
believe'. That has not only a stylistic significance; here
attention is urgently called to the fact that the content of the
Christian Confession is brought once more into a new light, and
that what now follows is not obviously connected with what goes
before. It is like taking a breath; it is the remarkable pause between
the Ascension and Whitsun.

The utterances of the third article are directed towards man.
While the first article speaks of God, the second of the God-man,
so now the third speaks of man. Here we must, of course, not
separate the three articles; we must understand them in their
unity. We are concerned with man who participates in the act of
God, and moreover participates actively. Man belongs to the
Creed. This is the unheard-of mystery which we are now approaching. There is a faith in man, so far as this man freely and
actively participates in the work of God. That this actually takes
place, is the work of the Holy Spirit, the work of God on earth,
which has its analogue in that hidden work of God, the outgoing
of the Spirit from the Father and the Son.

What is the meaning of this participation of man in the work
of God, of his free, active share? It would be comfortless if everything remained objective. There is also a subjective element;
and we may regard the modern exuberance of this subjective
element, which had already been introduced in the middle of the
seventeenth century, and was brought by Schleiermacher into

systematic order, as a strained attempt to bring the truth of the third article into force.

There is a general connexion of *all* men with Christ, and every man is His brother. He died for all man and rose for all men; so every man is the addressee of the work of Jesus Christ. That this is the case, is a promise for the whole of humanity. And it is the most important basis, and the only one which touches everything, for what we call humanity. He who has once realised the fact that God was made man cannot speak and act inhumanly.

But first of all, when we speak of the Holy Spirit, let us look not at all men, but at special men belonging in a special way to Jesus Christ. When we speak of the Holy Spirit, we have to do with the men who belong to Jesus Christ in the special way that they have the freedom to recognise His Word, His work, His message in a definite way and also to hope on their part the best for all men.

When we spoke of faith, we stressed the concept of freedom. Where the Spirit of the Lord is, there is freedom. If we wish to paraphrase the mystery of the Holy Spirit it is best to choose this concept. To receive the Spirit, to have the Spirit, to live in the Spirit means being set free and being permitted to live in freedom. Not all men are free. Freedom is not a matter of course and is not simply a predicate of human existence. All men are destined to freedom, but not all are in this freedom. Where the line of separation runs is hidden from us men. The Spirit bloweth where He listeth. It is indeed not a natural condition of man for him to have the Spirit; it will always be a distinction, a gift of God. What matters here is, quite simply, belonging to Jesus Christ. We are not concerned in the Holy Spirit with something different from Him and new. It was always an erroneous conception of the Holy Spirit, that so understood Him. The Holy Spirit is the Spirit of Jesus Christ. 'Of mine He shall take and give to you.' The Holy Spirit is nothing else than a certain relation of the Word to man. In the outpouring of the Holy Spirit at Whitsun, there is a movement—*pneuma* means wind—from Christ to man. He breathed on them: 'Receive ye the Holy Ghost!' Christians are those breathed upon by Christ. Therefore we can never in one respect speak soberly enough of the Holy Spirit. What is involved is the participation of man in the word and work of Christ.

But this simple thing is at the same time something supremely inconceivable. For this participation of man means active participation. Let us also ponder what this means in its true depth:

to be brought actively into the great hope of Jesus Christ which holds for all men, is truly not a matter of course. It is the answer to a question which is put to us afresh every morning. It involves the message of the Christian Church; and by my listening to this message it becomes my own task. This message is passed on to me too, as a Christian; I too have become the bearer of it. But thereby I am put into the position of having on my part to regard men, all men, quite differently from before; I can now no longer do otherwise than hope the best for all.

To have inner ears for the Word of Christ, to become thankful for His work and at the same time responsible for the message about Him and, lastly, to take confidence in men for Christ's sake —that is the freedom which we obtain, when Christ breathes on us, when He sends us His Holy Spirit. If He no longer lives in a historical or heavenly, a theological or ecclesiastical remoteness from me, if He approaches me and takes possession of me, the result will be that I hear, that I am thankful and responsible and that finally I may hope for myself and for all others; in other words, that I may live in a Christian way. It is a tremendously big thing and by no means a matter of course, to obtain this freedom. We must therefore every day and every hour pray *Veni Creator Spiritus* in listening to the word of Christ and in thankfulness. That is a closed circle. We do not 'have' this freedom; it is again and again given to us by God.

In the exposition of the first article of the Confession I said that creation is not a lesser miracle than the birth of Christ of the Virgin. And now thirdly I should like to say that the fact that there are Christians, men who have this freedom, is no lesser miracle than the birth of Jesus Christ of the Holy Spirit and the Virgin Mary, or than the creation of the world out of nothing. For if we remember what and who and how we are, we might well cry out, 'Lord, have mercy upon us'. For this miracle the disciples wait ten days after the Lord's Ascension into heaven. Not until after this pause does the outpouring of the Holy Spirit take place and with it the new community arises. There takes place a new act of God, which, like all God's acts, is a confirmation of the preceding ones. The Spirit cannot be separated from Jesus Christ. 'The Lord is the Spirit', says Paul.

Where men may receive and possess the Holy Spirit, it is of course a human experience and a human act. It is also a matter of the understanding and of the will and, I might indeed say, of the imagination. This too belongs to being a Christian. The *whole* man, right into the inmost regions of the so-called 'unconscious', is taken in claim. God's relation to man includes the whole of him. But there must be no misunderstanding: the Holy Spirit is not a form of the human spirit. Theology is traditionally reckoned to be one of the 'intellectual sciences'. It may good-humouredly let that pass. But the Holy Spirit is not identical with the human spirit, but He meets it. We certainly do not wish to degrade the human spirit—it is particularly necessary in the new Germany to cherish it a little—and even theologians should not turn aside in a Popish and haughty manner. But that freedom of Christian living does not come from the human spirit. No human capacities or possibilities or strivings of any kind can achieve this freedom.

When it happens that man obtains that freedom of becoming a hearer, a responsible, grateful, hopeful person, this is not because of an act of the human spirit, but solely because of the act of the Holy Spirit. So this is, in other words, a gift of God. It has to do with a new birth, with the Holy Spirit.

22

THE CHURCH, ITS UNITY, HOLINESS AND UNIVERSALITY

Since here and there through the Holy Spirit men meet with Jesus Christ and so also with one another, Christian community visibly arises and exists here and there. It is a form of the one, holy, universal people of God and a communion of holy men and works, in that it submits to sole rule by Jesus Christ, in whom it is founded, that it also aims to live solely in the fulfilment of its service as ambassador, that it recognises its goal solely in its hope, which is its limit.

WE must be brief in this section, which by rights ought to be very thoroughly treated. Our lecture hours are numbered. But perhaps there is no harm in that. To-day there is rather too much than too little said about the Church. There is something better: let us *be* the Church!

It would be great gain, could Luther's urgent desire have been carried out and the word 'congregation' had taken the place of the word 'Church'. Of course we may find in the word 'Church' what is good and true, since Church means *Kyriake Oikia*, the Lord's House; or, derived from *circa*, a circularly enclosed space. Both explanations are possible, but *ekklesia* certainly means congregation, a *coming together*, arising out of the summons to the national assembly which meets at the call of the messenger or else at the sound of the herald's trumpet.

A congregation is the coming together of those who belong to Jesus Christ through the Holy Spirit. We heard that special men belong in a special way to Jesus Christ. This takes place when men are called by the Holy Spirit to participation in Christ's word and work. This special membership has its analogue on the horizontal level in a membership of those men with one another. The outpouring of the Holy Spirit directly effects the coming together of these men. We cannot speak of the Holy Spirit—and that is why at this point the congregation immediately appears—without continuing *credo ecclesiam*, I believe in the

existence of the Church. And conversely, Woe to us, where we
think we can speak of the Church without establishing it wholly
on the work of the Holy Spirit. *Credo in Spiritum sanctum*, but not
Credo in ecclesiam. I believe in the Holy Spirit, but not in the
Church. Rather I believe in the Holy Spirit, and therefore also
in the existence of the Church, of the congregation. So then we
must eliminate all ideas of other human assemblies and societies
which have come into being, partly by nature, partly by history,
on the basis of agreements and arrangements. The Christian
congregation arises and exists neither by nature nor by historical
human decision, but as a divine *convocatio*. Those called together
by the work of the Holy Spirit assemble at the summons of their
King. Where the Church coincides with the natural living community, with, for example, that of the nation, the danger of a
misunderstanding always threatens. It cannot be formed by
men's hands; that is why the zealous, swift founding of Churches,
such as took place in America and also sometimes in Holland, is
a doubtful business. Calvin liked to apply to the Church a military
conception, that of *la compagnie des fidèles*. A company usually
comes together on the basis of a command and not on that of a
free agreement.

By men assembling here and there in the Holy Spirit there
arises here and there a visible Christian congregation. It is best
not to apply the idea of invisibility to the Church; we are all
inclined to slip away with that in the direction of a *civitas platonica*
or some sort of Cloud-cuckooland, in which the Christians are
united inwardly and invisibly, while the visible Church is de-
valued. In the Apostles' Creed it is not an invisible structure which
is intended but a quite visible coming together, which originates
with the twelve Apostles. The first congregation was a visible
group, which caused a visible public uproar. If the Church has
not this visibility, then it is not the Church. When I say congregation, I am thinking primarily of the concrete form of the congregation in a particular place. Of course each of these congregations
has its problems, such as the congregation of Rome, of Jerusalem,
etc. The New Testament never presents the Church apart from
these problems. At once the problem of variations in the individual
congregations crops up, which may lead to splits. All this belongs
to the visibility of the Church, which is the subject matter of the
second article. We believe the existence of the Church—which
means that we believe each particular congregation to be a

congregation of Christ. Take good note, that a parson who does
not believe that in this congregation of his, including those men
and women, old wives and children, Christ's congregation exists,
does not believe at all in the existence of the Church. *Credo
ecclesiam* means that I believe that here, at this place, in this
visible assembly, the work of the Holy Spirit takes place. By that
is not intended a deification of the creature; the Church is not the
object of faith, we do not believe *in* the Church; but we do believe that in this congregation the work of the Holy Spirit becomes
an event. The mystery of the Church is that for the Holy Spirit
it is not too small a thing to have such forms. Consequently, there
are in truth not many Churches but *one* Church in terms of this
or that *concrete* one, which should recognise itself as the one Church
and in all the others as well.

Credo unam ecclesiam: I believe one form of the one people of God
which has heard the voice of the Lord. There are also parlous
differences like those, for example, between our own and the
Roman Catholic Church, in which it is not simple to recognise
the one Church. But even there the Church is still more or less
recognisable. But first of all, Christians are simply summoned to
believe in God as the common origin, the common goal of the
Church to which they are called. We are not placed upon a
tower, from which we can survey all varieties of Churches; we
simply stand on the earth at a definite place and *there* is the
Church, the one Church. We believe in the unity of the Church,
in the unity of the congregations, if we believe in the existence of
our concrete Church. If we believe in the Holy Spirit in *this*
Church, then even in the worst case we are not absolutely separated from the other congregations. The truly ecumenical Christians are not those who trivialise the differences and flutter over
them; they are those who in their respective Churches are quite
concretely the Church. 'Where two or three are gathered together
in my name, there am I in their midst'—that is the Church. In
Him, despite all varieties in the individual congregations, we
shall somehow be bound up with one another.

'I believe one *holy* . . . Church.' What is the meaning of *sancta
ecclesia*? According to biblical usage of the term, it means 'set
apart'. And we think of the origin of the Church, of those called
out of the world. 'Church' will always signify a separation. We
heard that there are also natural and historical societies, but
that only the Christian congregation is the *ecclesia sancta*. It is

distinguished from all such societies because of its commission, its foundation and its goal.

'I believe one holy, *catholic* [universal] . . . Church'—the *ecclesia catholica*. The concept of Catholicity is tainted for us, because in this connexion we think of the Roman Catholics. But the Reformers undoubtedly made a claim upon this concept for themselves. What is involved is the one, holy and catholic people of God. Fundamentally the three concepts make the same assertion: *ecclesia catholica* means that through the whole of history the Church remains identical with itself. It cannot alter in its nature. There are, of course, different forms in the main Churches. There are also weaknesses, perversions, errors in all Churches. But there are not substantially different Churches. Their opposition could only be that of true and false Churches. We shall do well not to cast this opposition too swiftly and too often into the discussion.

The Church is the communion of the saints, *communio sanctorum*. Here there is a problem of exegesis: is the nominative *sancti* or *sancta*? I do not wish to decide the dispute, but just to ask whether there is not here intended a remarkable ambiguity in a deeper sense. For only when both interpretations are retained side by side, does the matter receive its full, good meaning. *Sancti* means not specially fine people, but, for example, people like the 'saints of Corinth', who were very queer saints. But these queer folk, to whom we too may belong, are *sancti*, that is, men set apart—for holy gifts and works, for *sancta*. The congregation is the place where God's word is proclaimed and the sacraments are solemnised and the fellowship of prayer takes place, not to mention the inward gifts and works, which are the meaning of these outward ones. So the *sancti* belong to the *sancta* and vice versa.

Let me recapitulate: *Credo ecclesiam* means that I believe that the congregation to which I belong, in which I have been called to faith and am responsible for my faith, in which I have my service, is the one, holy, universal Church. If I do not believe this here, I do not believe it at all. No lack of beauty, no 'wrinkles and spots' in this congregation may lead me astray. The thing involved here is an article of faith. There is no sense, when seeking after the 'true' congregation, in abandoning one's concrete congregation. Everywhere we are 'playing at man'. Of course, schism cannot be excluded; it may be objectively necessary.

But no schism will ever lead to 'playing at man' being dropped completely in the newly separated congregation of the Holy Spirit. When the Reformers came and the Roman Church remained behind the Reformed Church and separated from it, there was in action in the evangelical Church no spotless Church, either, it too was and is full of 'spots and wrinkles' to this very day. In faith I attest that the concrete congregation to which I belong and for the life of which I am responsible, is appointed to the task of making in this place, in this form, the one, holy, universal Church visible. By saying Yes to it, as to one which belongs with the other congregations by the Holy Spirit, I hope and expect that the one Holy Spirit of Jesus Christ will in it and through it attest also to others and confirm that in it the one, universal holy nature of the Church will become visible.

In the Nicene Creed a fourth is added to these three predicates of the Church, that I believe one, holy, catholic and *apostolic* Church. But this fourth one does not simply stand in a row with the other three expressions, but explains them. What is the meaning of Unity, Catholicity, Holiness? What distinguishes the congregation from all other societies of a natural or even of an historical kind? We can perhaps say that it is the *ecclesia apostolica* —that is, the Church founded on the witness of the Apostles— which transmits this witness, and which was constituted and will be constituted ever anew by the fact that it hears this testimony of the Apostles. We are faced with the complete fullness of the Church's existence and at the same time with a fullness of problems, to enter upon which we have neither time nor space left. But I will attempt to make visible along three lines, what apostolicity of the Church means.

Our opening sentence says that the Christian congregation is 'a communion of holy men and works, in that it submits to sole rule by Jesus Christ, in whom it is founded, that it also aims to live solely in the fulfilment of its service as ambassador, that it recognises its goal solely in its hope, which is its limit'. Here you see the three lines that are involved.

1. Where the Christian Church is, we are obviously connected in some form or other with Jesus Christ. This name indicates the unity, holiness and universality of the Church. Whether this basis and appeal to it takes place *de jure* is the question that must be put to every congregation in every place. Where the Apostolic Church is, the Church which hears and transmits the Apostles' testimony,

a definite sign will be living, a *nota ecclesiae*, that Jesus Christ, namely, is not only He from whom the Church derives, but that Christ is He that rules the congregation. He, and He alone! At no time and in no place is the Church an authority which upholds itself out of itself, but—and here follows an important principle with regard to Church governments—fundamentally the Church can be governed neither monarchically nor democratically. Here Jesus Christ rules alone, and any ruling of man can only represent this government of His. It must let itself be measured by that government. But Jesus Christ rules in His Word by the Holy Spirit. Church government is thus identical with Holy Scripture, for it witnesses to Him. So the Church must continually be occupied with the exposition and application of Scripture. Where the Bible becomes a dead book with a cross on the cover and gilt edging, the Church rule of Jesus Christ is slumbering. There the Church is no longer the one holy universal Church, but the threat is there of the breaking in of what is unholy and separatist. Of course even this 'Church' will call on the name of Jesus Christ. But it is not words but reality which matters; and such a Church will not be in a position to bring reality into action.

2. The life of the one holy universal Church is determined by the fact that it is the fulfilment of the service as ambassador enjoined upon it. The Church lives as other communities live, but in its Church service its nature appears—proclamation of the Word of God, administration of the Sacraments, a more or less developed liturgy, the application of a Church law (the thesis of R. Sohm is a fantastic business, for even the first congregation had at least a Church-law order, namely Apostles and congregation), and lastly theology. The great problem, which the Church has again and again to answer, is this—what happens in and by all these functions? Is it a question of edification? Is the blessedness of individuals or of all involved? Is it the cultivation of religious living, or quite objectively an order (in accord with an ontological conception of the Church) which must simply be achieved as the *opus Dei*? Where the life of the Church is exhausted in self-serving, it smacks of death; the decisive thing has been forgotten, that this whole life is lived only in the exercise of what we called the Church's service as ambassador, proclamation, *kerygma*. A Church that recognises its commission will neither desire nor be able to petrify in any of its functions, to be the Church for its own sake. There is the 'Christ-believing group'; but

this group is *sent out*: 'Go and preach the Gospel!' It does not say, 'Go and celebrate services!' 'Go and edify yourselves with the sermon!' 'Go and celebrate the Sacraments!' 'Go and present yourselves in a liturgy, which perhaps repeats the heavenly liturgy!' 'Go and devise a theology which may gloriously unfold like the *Summa* of St Thomas!' Of course, there is nothing to forbid all this; there may exist very good cause to do it all; but nothing, nothing at all for its own sake! In it all the one thing must prevail: 'Proclaim the Gospel to every creature!' The Church runs like a herald to deliver the message. It is not a snail that carries its little house on its back and is so well off in it, that only now and then it sticks out its feelers, and then thinks that the 'claim of publicity' has been satisfied. No, the Church lives by its commission as herald; it is *la compagnie de Dieu.* Where the Church is living, it must ask itself whether it is serving this commission or whether it is a purpose in itself? If the second is the case, then as a rule it begins to smack of the 'sacred', to affect piety, to play the priest and to mumble. Anyone with a keen nose will smell it and find it dreadful! Christianity is not 'sacred'; rather there breathes in it the fresh air of the Spirit. Otherwise it is not Christianity. For it is an out-and-out 'worldly' thing open to all humanity: 'Go into all the world and proclaim the Gospel to every creature.'

3. And now the last point, that where the Church is, there it has an aim, the kingdom of God. This goal of the Church is bound to constitute a continuous restlessness for the men in the Church, whose action stands in no relation to the greatness of this goal. We must not allow Christian existence, that is the existence of the Church, and theological existence, to be spoiled by this. It may well happen that we might want to drop the hand that is put to the plough, when we compare the Church with its goal. We may often have a distaste for the whole of Church life. If you do not know this oppression, if you simply feel well inside the Church's walls, you have certainly not seen the real dynamic in this matter. In the Church we may be just like a bird in a cage which is always hitting against the bars. Something bigger is at stake than our bit of preaching and liturgy! But where the Apostolic Church is alive, one knows, indeed, this longing, we long for the mansion made ready for us, but we don't make off, we don't simply run away. We do not let ourselves be hindered, by the hope of the kingdom, from standing as a private soldier

in the *compagnie de Dieu* and so making for the goal. The limit
is set us by the goal. If we really hope for the kingdom of God,
then we can also endure the Church in its pettiness. Then we
shall not be ashamed to discover in the concrete congregation
the one holy universal Church, and then every individual will not
be ashamed of his particular confession. The Christian hope,
which is the most revolutionary thing we are capable of thinking
and beside which all other revolutions are mere blank cartridges,
is a disciplined hope. It points man to his limitations: there you
may hold out. The Kingdom of God is *coming*, so you must not
begin the flight to the kingdom of God. Take your place and be
in your place as a true *minister verbi divini*. You can be a revolutionary, but you can also be a conservative. Where this contrast
between revolutionary and conservative is united in one man,
where he may be at once quite restless and quite at rest, where
he may be with the others in that way in the congregation,
in which the members recognise each other in longing and
in humility in the light of the divine humour, he will do what
he has to do. In this light all our Church action is allowed and
in fact commended. So the Church, waiting and hurrying, goes
to meet the coming of the Lord.

23

THE FORGIVENESS OF SINS

The Christian man looks back and in spite of his sin receives the witness through the Holy Spirit and through holy baptism of the death of Jesus Christ and so of the justification of his own life. His faith in the latter is founded on the fact that God Himself, by taking man's place in Jesus Christ, has taken over the unconditional responsibility for his way.

THIS is the way of the Christian man, which is constituted through God's grace and which has its place in the congregation. We must therefore under no circumstances separate what we have now to hear of, forgiveness of sins, resurrection of the flesh and eternal life, from the fact that God by the Holy Spirit acts so that there are men who listen and that a congregation arises. The way of the Christian is derived from the forgiveness of sins and leads to the resurrection of the body and eternal life. This whence and whither of the Christian man is really and substantially concentrated at a single point. This point is the centre of the second article, the passion and action of Jesus Christ. We belong together with Him in the Holy Spirit. We are His congregation, and all that is ours is originally and properly His. We live by what is His. We must not fall away from this centring of all truth. Forgiveness of sins, resurrection, eternal life are not something outside Christ, but are God's action in Him. He, the One, lightens, and the Christian man moves in His light. What distinguishes the Christian man is that he stands in this cone of light which proceeds from Christ. But this existence of his in the light is not a selfish purpose, but the Christian man moves in this light, in order to be a light himself. God so loved the world that He gave His only-begotten Son. Christians are messengers in Christ's stead. But here in the congregation it is recognised, it is seen and experienced, what Christ is for man, for all men, in order that witness may be borne from here.

I believe in the forgiveness of sins—this is the point at which the Christian man obviously looks *back* on the way from which he originates. Not just in the moment of his 'conversion', but it is always the case that when the Christian looks back, he is looking at the forgiveness of sins. That is the event that confronts him and sets him up, that and nothing else. There is nothing added to it, like forgiveness of sin *and* my experience or forgiveness of sins *and* my achievement! What in retrospect we know about ourselves, can always be only that we live by forgiveness. We are beggars, truly enough.

If forgiveness of sin means all that lies behind us, then a judgment is thereby passed upon our life. There is no merit at all, that of thankfulness, say, in which I have offered all sorts of things to the dear God. I have been a fighter! I have been a theologian! Have perhaps actually written books! No, that will not do. All that we were and achieved will be subject to the judgment that it was sin. And sin means transgression, deviation. And if there was something else, it was always the thing that came from above, of which we have no cause to boast, even though it be the mercy of God. Every day we ought to begin, we may begin with the confession: 'I believe in the forgiveness of sins.' In the brief hour of our death we shall still have nothing else to say. Perhaps we can best clarify the concept of forgiveness or *remissio*, as that something has been recorded in writing, namely, our life; and now a great stroke is drawn through the whole. It deserves to be stroked out and—thank God!—it will be stroked out. In spite of my sin, I may now accept a testimony that my sin is not reckoned to me. I cannot myself remove this from myself. Sin means man's eternal lostness. How should we manage to remove that ourselves? That I have sinned means that I am a sinner.

And against all this there goes forth the witness of the Holy Spirit, the witness of the heard Word of God and the witness of baptism. For the relevance of holy baptism is this, that we may our whole life long think upon the fact that we are baptised; just as Luther in temptation took a chalk and wrote on the table, *baptizatus sum*. Baptism concerns me completely, quite independently of whether I always perceive the witness of the Holy Spirit with the same liveliness. There is something wrong with our perception. There is a rise and fall in it; there are times when for me the word is not living, and that is where the fact may interpose, that I am baptised. Once in my life a sign has been established, which I may hold on to even at a time when the witness of the Holy Spirit does not reach me. Just as I was born, I was once baptised. As a baptised person I become a witness to myself. Baptism can attest nothing but what the Holy Spirit attests, but as a baptised person I may myself be the witness to the Holy Spirit and restore myself by this witness. Baptism recalls me to the service of witness, since it recalls me to daily repentance. It is a signal set up in our life. As the motions of swimming come again to one who has fallen into the water, so baptism recalls us to witness.

But this witness is the Word of God to us, saying: You, O man, with your sin belong utterly, as Jesus Christ's property, to the realm of the inconceivable mercy of God, who will not regard us as those who live as they live and act as they act, but says to us, 'You are justified'. For Me you are no longer the sinner, but where you are there stands Another. I look at this Other. And if you are anxious, how you are to make repentance, just let it be said to you: 'For you repentance has been made.' And if you ask, what service I can give, how I can frame my life in fellowship with God, let the answer come to you that the expiation for your life has already been made and your communion with God completed. Your act, O son of man, can only consist in your accepting this situation, that God sees you anew and adopts you anew in His light, as the creature you are. 'We are buried with him by baptism into death' (Romans 6. 4). Baptism is a representation of Christ's death in the midst of our life. It tells us that when Christ has been dead and buried we too have been dead and buried, we the transgressors and sinners. As one baptised you may see yourself as dead. The forgiveness of sins rests on the fact that this dying took place at that time on Golgotha. Baptism tells you that that death was also your death.

God Himself has in Jesus Christ stepped into man's place. We think once more of our assertion that the reconciliation is an exchange. God now takes over the responsibility for us. We are now His property, and He has the disposal of us. Our own unworthiness affects us no longer. We may now live by the fact that He does it. Which means not a passive but an extremely active existence. If we may use a figure, we may think of a child drawing an object. He does not succeed with it. Then the teacher sits down in the child's place and draws the same object. The child stands beside him and just looks on, as the teacher makes the fine drawing in his own exercise-book. That is justification—God accomplishing in our place what we cannot accomplish. I have been pushed off the tiny form; and now if there is still anything to be said against me, why, it no longer concerns me, but Him who is sitting in my place. And as for those who have to complain about me, the devil and his cohorts and one's dear fellow men, should they dare to rise against me, why, He is sitting in my place. That is my situation. Thus I am acquitted and may be wholly joyful, because the accusations cease to come home to me. The righteousness of Jesus Christ is now my righteousness. That is the forgiveness of sins. 'How art thou righteous before God? Only by faith in Jesus Christ' (Question 60, *Heidelberg Catechism*). This is how the Reformation saw the matter and expressed it. God grant that we may learn how to acquire once more the fullness of truth and life which results from it.

And now we must not say that it is not enough to live by forgiveness 'alone'. This objection has been raised against the Creed and strengthened against the Reformers. What folly! As though just this, the forgiveness of sins, were not the only thing by which we live, the power of all powers! As though everything were not said in that phrase! It is precisely when we are aware that 'God is for me', that we are in the true sense *responsible*. For from that standpoint and from that alone is there a real ethic, have we a criterion of good and evil. So living by forgiveness is never by any means passivity, but Christian living in full activity. Whether we prefer to describe it as great freedom or as strict discipline, as piety or as true worldliness, as private morality or as social morality, whether we regard this life under the sign of the great hope or under the sign of daily patience, in any case we live solely by forgiveness. Here lies the distinction between the Christian and the heathen, the Christian and the Jew. What does not pass over this sharp ridge of forgiveness of sins, or grace, is not Christian. By this we shall be judged, about this the Judge will one day put the question, Did you live by grace, or did you set up gods for yourself and perhaps want to become one yourself? Have you been a faithful servant, who has nothing to boast of? In that case you are accepted; for then you have surely been merciful as well and have forgiven your debtors; then you have surely also comforted others and been a light, then your works have surely been good works, works which flow from the forgiveness of sins. The question about these works is the Judge's question, which we have to face.

24

THE RESURRECTION OF THE BODY
AND THE LIFE EVERLASTING

A Christian looks forward and in spite of his death receives the witness of the Holy Spirit and of the Lord's Supper to the resurrection of Jesus Christ and thus to the completion of his own life. His faith in this is founded on the fact that, since man is permitted to take in Jesus Christ God's place, there is bestowed upon him unconditional participation in the glory of God.

A CHRISTIAN looks back, we said in the preceding opening statement. A Christian looks forward, we now say. This looking back and looking forward constitute the life of a Christian, the *vita humana Christiana*, the life of a man who has received the Holy Spirit, who may live in the congregation and is called to be in it a light of the world.

A man looks forward. We take a turn, as it were, of 180 degrees: behind us lies our sin and before us death, dying, the coffin, the grave, the end. The man who does not take it seriously that we are looking to that end, the man who does not realise what dying means, who is not terrified at it, who has perhaps not enough joy in life and so does not know the fear of the end, who has not yet understood that this life is a gift of God, who has no trace of envy at the longevity of the patriarchs, who were not only one hundred but three hundred and four hundred and more years old, the man who, in other words, does not grasp the beauty of this life, cannot grasp the significance of 'resurrection'. For this word is the answer to death's terror, the terror that this life some day comes to an end, and that this end is the horizon of our existence. 'In the midst of life we are girt about with death. . . .' Human existence is an existence under this threat, marked by this end, by this contradiction continually raised against our existence: you can not live! You believe in Jesus Christ and can only believe and not see. You stand before God and would like to enjoy yourself and may enjoy yourself, and yet must experience every day how your sin is new every morning. There is peace, and yet only the

peace which can be confirmed amid struggle. Here we understand, and yet at the same time we understand so overwhelmingly
little. There is life, and yet but life in the shadow of death. We
are beside each other, and yet must one day separate from one
another. Death sets its seal upon the whole; it is the wages of sin.
The account is closed, the coffin and corruption are the last word.
The contest is decided, and decided against us. Such is death.

And now the Christian man looks forward. What is the meaning
of the Christian hope in this life? A life after death? An event
apart from death? A tiny soul which, like a butterfly, flutters
away above the grave and is still preserved somewhere, in order
to live on immortally? That was how the heathen looked on the
life after death. But that is not the Christian hope. 'I believe in
the resurrection of the body.' Body in the Bible is quite simply
man, man, moreover, under the sign of sin, man laid low. And to
this man it is said, Thou shalt rise again. Resurrection means not
the continuation of this life, but life's completion. To this man
a 'Yes' is spoken which the shadow of death cannot touch. In
resurrection our life is involved, we men as we are and are situated. *We* rise again, no one else takes our place. 'We shall be
changed' (1 Cor. 15); which does not mean that a quite different
life begins, but that '*this* corruptible must put on incorruption,
and this mortal put on immortality'. Then it will be manifest that
'death is swallowed up in victory'. So the Christian hope affects
our whole life: this life of ours will be completed. That which is
sown in dishonour and weakness will rise again in glory and power.
The Christian hope does not lead us away from this life; it is
rather the uncovering of the truth in which God sees our life. It
is the conquest of death, but not a flight into the Beyond. The
reality of this life is involved. Eschatology, rightly understood, is
the most practical thing that can be thought. In the eschaton
the light falls from above into our life. We await this light. 'We
bid you hope', said Goethe. Perhaps even he knew of this light.
The Christian message, at any rate, confidently and comfortingly
proclaims hope in this light.

It is true that we cannot give ourselves, or persuade ourselves
that we have, the hope that our life will be completed. It must be
believed, in death's despite. The man who does not know what
death is does not know either what resurrection is. It needs the
witness of the Holy Spirit, the witness of the Word of God proclaimed and heard in Scripture, the witness of the risen Jesus

Christ, in order to believe that there shall be light and that this light shall complete our uncompleted life. The Holy Spirit who speaks to us in Scripture tells us that we may live in this great hope.

The Lord's Supper ought to be more firmly regarded from the Easter standpoint, than is generally the case. It is not primarily a mourning or funeral meal, but the anticipation of the marriage feast of the Lamb. The Supper is a joyous meal: the eating of His, Jesus Christ's, flesh and the drinking of His blood is meat and drink unto life eternal in the midst of our life. We are guests at His table and so no longer separated from Himself. Thus in this sign the witness of His meal is united to the witness of the Holy Spirit. It tells us really, you shall not die but live, and proclaim the Lord's works! *You!* We are guests at the Lord's Table, which is not only an image; it is an event. 'Whosoever believeth on me, hath the life eternal.' Your death is put to death. You are in fact already dead. The terror you face you have already completely behind you. You may live as a guest at this table. You may go in the strength of this food forty days and forty nights. In this strength it is possible. Let this prevail, that you have drunk and eaten; let all that is deadly round about you be conquered. Do not nurse your sorrow tenderly; do not make a little garden of it with an overhanging weeping willow! 'We do but make the cross and pain the greater by our melancholy.' We are called to a quite different situation. 'If we died with Christ, we *believe* that we shall also live with Him' (Rom. 6. 8). The man who believes that is already beginning here and now to live the complete life.

The Christian hope is the seed of eternal life. In Jesus Christ I am no longer at the point at which I can die; in Him our body is already in heaven (Question 49, *Heidelberg Catechism*). Since we may receive the testimony of the Lord's Supper, we already live here and now in anticipation of the eschaton, when God will be all in all.

71 72 73   12 11 10

2)